The Positive Thinking Workbook for Women

Real and Proven Ways to Keep a Positive Attitude No Matter What, Build Self-Confidence and Be Happy Every Day

Victoria Tyler

© Copyright 2021 - Victoria Tyler - All rights reserved.

The content contained within this book may not be reproduced, duplicated or transmitted without di-rect written permission from the author or the publisher.
Under no circumstances will any blame or legal re-sponsibility be held against the publisher, or au-thor, for any damages, reparation, or monetary loss due to the information contained within this book; either directly or indirectly.

Legal Notice:
This book is copyright protected. This book is only for personal use. You cannot amend, distribute, sell, use, quote or paraphrase any part, or the con-tent within this book, without the consent of the author or publisher.

Disclaimer Notice:
Please note the information contained within this document is for educational and entertainment purposes only. All effort has been executed to pre-sent accurate, up to date, and reliable, complete in-formation. No warranties of any kind are declared or implied. Readers acknowledge that the author is not engaging in the rendering of legal, financial, medical or professional advice.

TABLE OF CONTENTS

Introduction	4
Are you thinking negatively?	8
Identify your struggles	24
Practicing Gratitude	35
Build Self-Esteem	63
Encouraging Women	99
Negative Thoughts vs Positive Thoughts	116
Master the Art of Meditation	128
The World With Kindness	137
Practice Self-Love	145
Conclusion	145
Author's Note	161

INTRODUCTION

Welcome to Positive Thinking for Women. First, I would like to congratulate you on starting your journey towards embracing a more positive outlook on life. The fact that you have decided to read this book shows your willingness to learn and grow. It shows that you are not afraid to look within yourself and connect with yourself on a deeper level. You are a fierce woman who knows that she deserves to be happy; so well done for taking that first step!

You might be a little skeptical about how easy it can be to change one's mindset. Your doubt is understandable - after all, changing one's thinking is not a piece of cake, especially when you have been thinking a certain way for the majority of your life. You are most likely aware that your mindset needs to shift to a more positive space; however, it is normal not to be able to pinpoint what exactly needs to change - and how. Thinking one way can make you feel as though your current mindset is working for you, especially if you have experienced some wins with the way you think.

It is normal to question whether it is worth changing your outlook on life, because of course, instilling drastic change within is not a walk in the park. It is natural to feel hesitant or nervous because you are so used to your thought patterns: it is familiar ground. You might be nervous about how you will manage the changes, and if they will make you feel worse than you already might be feeling now; however, it is important to remember that working towards positive change will reap great benefits in your life.

As a woman, there are so many responsibilities you need to face every day, and quite frankly it can get exhausting. The world has evolved to a place in which every single aspect has a certain benchmark to be considered successful; and if anyone falls short, they are deemed not good enough. Unfortunately, women are not immune to these expectations. Whether it be regarding beauty, finances, career, health, childcare, education or any other aspect of life, women feel the pressure from society to prove themselves and show they are capable and worthy.

As you know, it can feel miserable to have your capabilities doubted, especially when you know you are doing your best. Add in prejudice, discrimination, and oppression, and you have a recipe for misery and declining mental health. For generations, women have had to bear the brunt of unequal treatment in society, and this has taken its toll on their wellbeing. It is understandable that with the pressures of daily life as well as facing microaggressions in society, a woman is bound to lose hope and adopt a cynical outlook on life.

While the world is moving towards a place where women are being recognized and treated as equals, there is still a constant struggle in large parts of the world. Women are strong, capable and beautiful beings that have every right to be treated fairly. Remember these words: you are an amazing woman that can shine in the world. It is now time to take matters into your own hands and show the world how amazing you truly are, starting with changing your mindset to a more positive one.

Whatever you have gone through in your life, you will be able to heal as you start to adopt a more positive way of thinking. Throughout the course of this workbook, you will learn how to shift your mindset to one that will benefit you, and with this new mindset you will be able to take actionable steps towards living a life of happiness, equality, and success. Through a combination of theoretical concepts and exercises, you will work your way through the workbook and gain the knowledge needed to change your outlook to one that brings you light in a dark world.

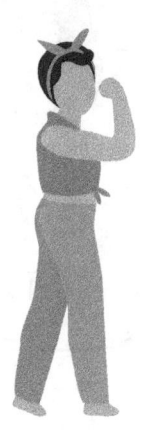

No matter how hard life tries to bring you down, your new and positive mindset will spring you back up and show you just how strong you really are. If you are already in a good place in your life, adopting a positive mindset will help you recognize how great your life is, and it will empower you to reach for more happiness. Thinking positively will be your path toward living a fulfilling life and being happy, and that is exactly what all women deserve.

PART 1
SELF-REFLECTION

CHAPTER 1:
ARE YOU THINKING NEGATIVELY?

Have you ever had a thought come across your mind one minute and then the next minute you are suddenly an anxiety-ridden mess curled up in bed under the covers? Ever wonder how a simple thought has the power to make you feel so many negative emotions? Most of the time, it is due to unhelpful and negative thinking patterns. In reality, life might be heading in a certain direction; however, your mind makes you believe that life is hurtling down another direction that is harmful to you. In actuality, it is your mind that is harming you more than life itself.

The goal of this workbook is to steer you in the right direction to thinking positively, which means you will need to identify areas in your thinking that might be bringing you down. This can be difficult to do not knowing what is defined as negative. You might believe that your thinking style is protecting you from harm or preparing you for the worst; however, most times this is just your mind's way of justifying the negative thought patterns because it might not even realize that it is an unhealthy form of thinking. There may have been times when thinking negatively might have actually helped protect you from certain things; however, most of the time thinking negatively harms you.

Negative thought patterns can take you to some dark places when your life in reality might not warrant such thoughts. In order to grow from these thought patterns, it is imperative to first identify what kinds of negative thoughts you usually have and when they present themselves. It is also important to recognize how you react to negative thoughts. For example, if you have been studying hard for an exam and after taking the exam got a B+, you might deem yourself to be a failure. A B+ is a good grade! However, thinking negatively, your mind will think that any grade that falls short of your expectation (which was an A+) is a complete defeat.

Thinking negatively in this case has convinced you that if something is not perfect or does not go the way you want, that means it is a total failure, and there is no good to seeing that situation. If your thought patterns were healthy, you would have instead recognized that you did your best and that a B+ is still a great achievement! You would take ownership of the small wins, even though you did not gain what you wanted to gain initially.

This negative thought pattern is common among people who expect things to go perfectly or according to plan every single time. They have very high expectations; and if anything falls short, then the person is unable to see the positives in the situation. One tiny blunder can make the entire situation seem doomed, when in actuality it is just a small blip in the plan. Thinking negatively in this way can leave a person feeling constantly unhappy because life does not always go according to plan and it is important to take things as they come and accept some of the shortfalls.

Sometimes, there is beauty in things not working out the way you wanted them to because it could be working out in a form that would be even better for you. Being unable to see the situation with all the information and only seeing the negative will fuel you to feel negative emotions and push you to behave in ways that are not beneficial to you or to other people. This is not to say that if something truly warrants an emotional response but you do not feel a certain way, of course, you can. However, it is important to view the situation from a holistic point of view with all the facts and then frame your thoughts accordingly. Making mountains out of molehills by filtering out some information rarely ever makes things better, and you will face the brunt of the pain.

Can you think of a time when you made a situation bigger than it needed to be? Write it down.

_____

_____

_____

_____

Piggy-backing onto this, there may have been times when you have been presented with an alternative option to what you initially wanted which could actually benefit you, but because it was not what you wanted in the first place, you were not able to see the positives in the option. Looking at life through a dark filter will make you miss out on some pretty wonderful things that life has to offer you. Sometimes it is so automatic that you do not even realize your mind is filtering information.

Thinking negatively prompts you to only look at the negative parts of a situation so that it can fit the narrative you have in your head about it. If you predict that something is not going to work out in your favor, you will look at only the aspects of the situation that prove that theory right, disregarding the other aspects that provide more holistic information and possibly another outcome.

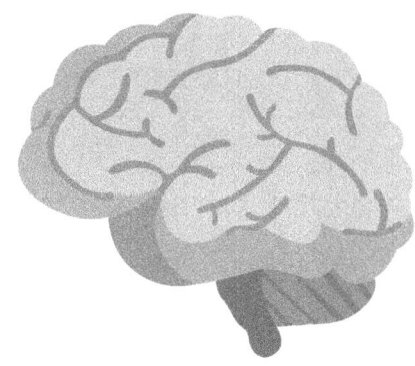
Your mind conveniently ignores other information and focuses on details that can prove your negative theory. In the world of psychology, this is called confirmation bias: you look for only relevant information that will confirm the theory you are cooking up and ignore any contradictory information that might be presented. By constantly doing this, you start to believe that you "know" the outcome of every situation will be negative and entertain negative thinking to "prepare" yourself for the worst - all because you sieved out the positives and only added the negatives into the recipe.

Every situation in life has some grey areas, and it is important to take into account all of the aspects to accurately judge the outcome, instead of making assumptions based on only the negative aspects that conveniently fit the negative narrative.

Think back to a time when you filtered out the positives from a situation and only looked at the negatives. Write down what happened.

_____

_____

_____

_____

_____

_____

Thinking negatively also makes you predict negative outcomes. Even if there are countless pieces of evidence that something might actually work out the way you want it to, your negative thought patterns will conjure up a reason why it might fail. Your mind probably wants to prepare you for the worst to spare you the brunt of disappointment if it were to not work out; however, doing this for every single situation in life makes you a cynic and does not leave room for you to have positive emotions or thoughts. You almost become a negative fortune-teller, who only predicts bad outcomes no matter what your crystal ball presents.

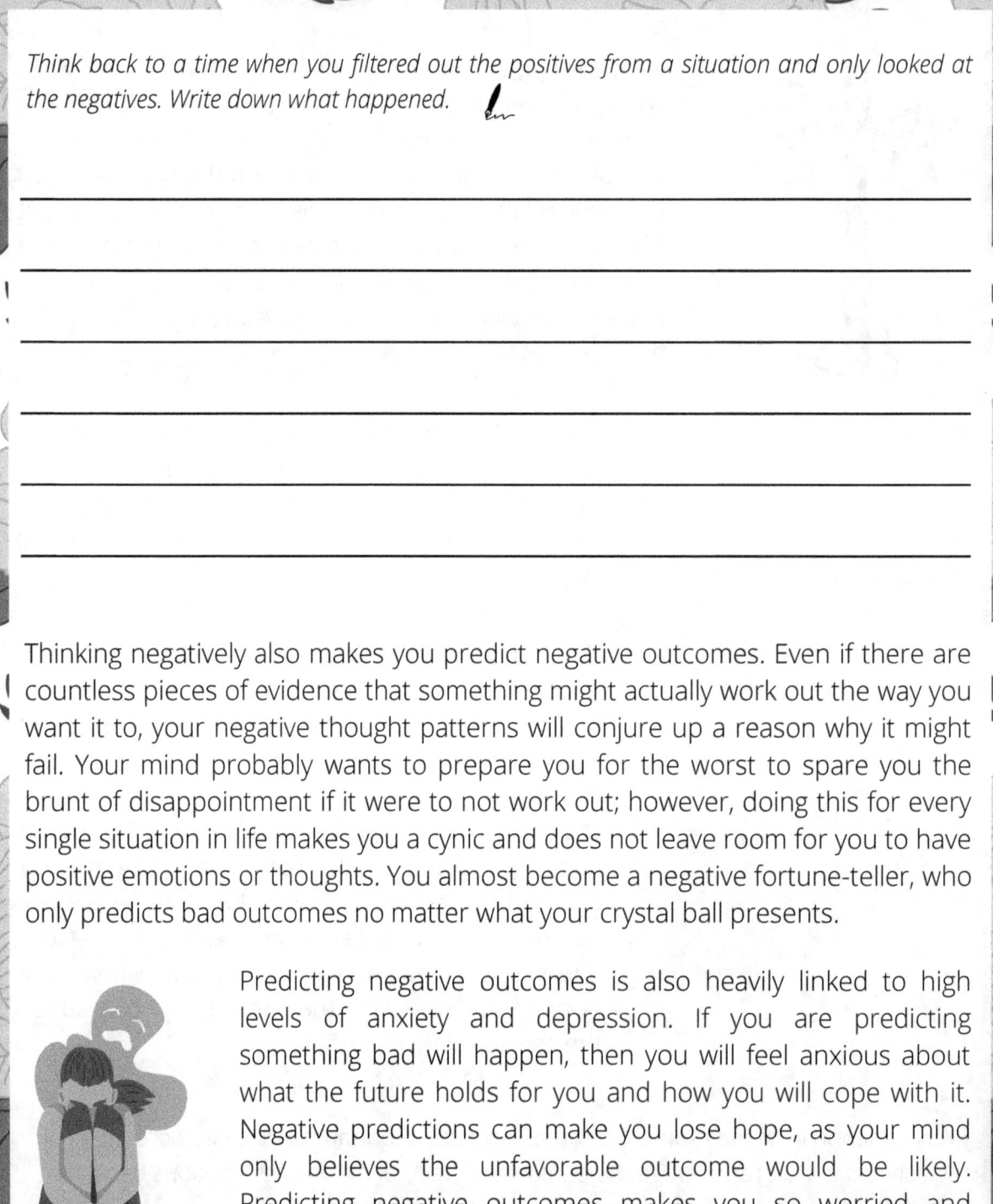

Predicting negative outcomes is also heavily linked to high levels of anxiety and depression. If you are predicting something bad will happen, then you will feel anxious about what the future holds for you and how you will cope with it. Negative predictions can make you lose hope, as your mind only believes the unfavorable outcome would be likely. Predicting negative outcomes makes you so worried and depressed about the future that you miss out on the present, which further affects your mental wellbeing.

Not being present in the current moment due to anxiety and depression regarding the future makes you think, feel, and behave in ways that correspond to that negative outcome you are predicting without it even happening. In some cases, the way you behave might result in a self-fulfilling prophecy in which the outcome you are predicting comes true due to some actions you take, whereas if you did not think negatively and did not behave in that way, that negative outcome would not have been likely to happen.

Thinking negatively about the future attracts negativity into your life. When you are putting negative vibes out into the universe, you are more likely to attract negativity from the universe as well. Since you do not know what the future holds for you, why not put out positive vibes into the universe and see what happens? That way, you are not bringing yourself down in the process and instead are keeping a positive attitude until you see the results.

When was the last time you predicted a negative outcome that did not end up coming true? Write it down.

_____

_____

_____

_____

_____

_____

_____

_____

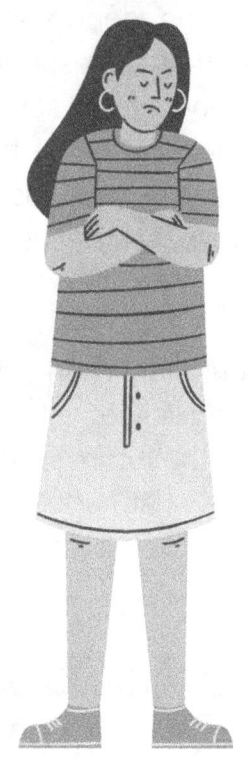

Thinking negatively fills you up with despair and anger. You start to truly believe that nothing good will ever happen to you, and it starts to overpower your sense of self-worth. Thinking and acting as if your life will never be filled with happiness will unconsciously ingrain into your mind that you are not worthy of happiness. The thoughts you have play a major role in your self-esteem and self-worth. If you keep telling yourself that nothing good is going to happen to you, then you will start to believe that you do not deserve good things. Why should you tell yourself that though? You, as much as anybody else in the world, deserve to be happy, successful, and loved. The only person who can convince you that you deserve a good life is you. Your inner voice is the most important one; and if your inner voice keeps spewing negativity, then you will be unable to see just how amazing you are and that you deserve happiness.

Having a low sense of self-worth makes you feel less confident about multiple aspects of your life and as a result, it can slow you down from achieving the goals you have set for yourself. If you were to think positively and say uplifting things to yourself, your mindset would shift and you would be more hopeful about all the great things you can achieve and you will feel more motivated to work towards your goals. Low self-esteem affects how you perceive yourself. and it is unfortunate because it makes you amplify your weaknesses (that might be totally fixable or might not even be weaknesses) and disregard your favorable traits. Having low self-esteem paints a skewed picture of yourself in your mind which only hurts you in the long-run.

What sorts of thoughts do you usually have? Are they mainly positive or negative?

_____
_____
_____
_____
_____
_____

Imagine a scenario in which you are due for a promotion. You have been working super hard and have put in the time and effort to ensure that you have proven how worthy you are of being given the next big opportunity at work. You also know that someone else who is just as worthy is also competing for the same promotion. In this situation, what thoughts would go through your head? Be honest with yourself and write them down.

_____
_____
_____
_____
_____
_____
_____

If you wrote down thoughts that were more negative, this shows that you have a tendency to underestimate yourself and predict negative outcomes, even though there is a 50/50 chance that things could go your way. Your mind chooses to look at the negative outcome instead of the positive outcome.

If you are still not convinced that thinking negatively can severely impact your life, there are quite a few side effects that should change your mind. Firstly, negative thought patterns can make you miss golden opportunities. For example, if you are extremely interested in acting and if you see an ad calling people to audition for a role in a well-known play, your negative thinking might cause you to shy away from it. How so? Your mind might convince you that you will not be good enough, you might embarrass yourself, or you simply do not have the time to do it. Your thoughts will comprise of all the reasons you should not go for that audition and because you trust the negative voice inside of you, you will listen to it and not go for that audition. Unfortunately, you miss the opportunity to engage in an activity you genuinely enjoy and potentially miss being chosen for the role that will make you shine on stage!

By getting stuck in negative thoughts, you miss opportunities in life that could actually make your life more fulfilling. Even something as simple as enjoying a meal: you could be eating your favorite food but your mind will keep telling you about all the calories that you might be ingesting, and as a result you do not get to enjoy the opportunity of eating that delicious meal. Any opportunity that makes you feel happier gets shot down with negative thoughts, which can make you feel miserable.

What sorts of thoughts do you usually have? Are they mainly positive or negative?

_____

_____

_____

_____

_____

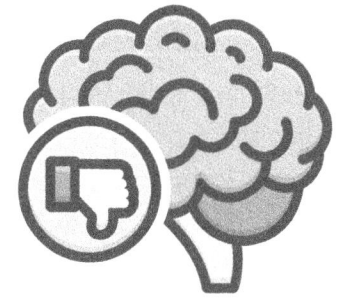 Negativity can also deeply impact your relationships! Whether it is a friendship, a romantic relationship, a professional relationship or a familial relationship, negative thoughts can cause you to behave in ways that hamper your bond with the person. Looking at romantic relationships in particular, you might be in a relationship with a person who truly cares for and loves but has to juggle a hectic work schedule.

Negativity can also deeply impact your relationships! Whether it is a friendship, a romantic relationship, a professional relationship or a familial relationship, negative thoughts can cause you to behave in ways that hamper your bond with the person. Looking at romantic relationships in particular, you might be in a relationship with a person who truly cares for and loves but has to juggle a hectic work schedule.

A person who does not indulge in negative thought processes will understand that their partner's work schedule is independent of their love for them, and that even though they are busy, the partner is trying their best to make the relationship work. However, if you think negatively, you might assume your partner does not want to spend time with you or you might think back to a situation in the past in which they could not get out of work to spend time with you and use this against them to make them feel guilty, which will result in a conflict. Negative thinking can make you misinterpret things in your relationship, which can put strain on the relationship. There is only so much a person can do to reassure you that your relationship with them is solid: it can get exhausting to constantly hear negativity from a partner when you are trying your best to keep the relationship afloat.

Thinking negatively makes you amplify your own internal struggles which you end up projecting onto the other person. For instance, if you struggle with gratitude and cannot see the good things in your life, you might project this onto the other person and tell them that they are ungrateful and do not appreciate you.

Your own faults become the other person's faults, and as a result, you make the other person feel as though they are not good enough to maintain the relationship they have with you. Negative thoughts amplify the other person's faults and make them feel worse than they already do, and can actually push them away from you. If someone were constantly blaming you for things you did not mean to do or were consistently pointing out your flaws, would you want to spend time with them?

It is human nature to want to distance yourself from people who make you feel bad about yourself and create a negative space around you. Put yourself in someone else's shoes and think about how your words might affect them. You probably do not have the intention of hurting them, but thinking negatively results in speaking negatively and that can hamper any type of relationship or friendship.

If you are someone who does not express your thoughts and emotions as easily as others, thinking negatively can be detrimental to your relationships. For example, if you have a negative thought that your partner might be interested in someone they work with and this makes you feel insecure, keeping that inside of you will eat you up alive. Granted, not all thoughts need to be entertained, especially if they are intrusive like this, but if it is really bothersome and you need some reassurance, you should speak to your partner about it.

Healthy relationships are formed on the basis of honest and open communication; expressing that negative thought and laying your fears out on the table can be beneficial for you and your partner, because then you are giving your partner the opportunity to put your fears to rest and show you how much they care for you.

By hoarding these negative thoughts, you start to feel insecure in the relationship and make assumptions about the other person that could very well not be even remotely true. Negative thinking can make your mind go to some dark places and it is essential that you recognize these thoughts and try to reframe them so that they do not have any negative implications on the relationship.

Think back to your friendships and relationships. Have your negative thoughts ever interfered with the stability of any of them? In what ways? Write down 2 examples.

_____

_____

_____

_____

Being unable to adopt a positive mindset means that you are living in a mindset that does not give you hope or happiness. A negative mindset attracts more negativity into your life. If you do not have hope that your career will take off or that you will be recognized for an accomplishment, then it is possible that what you are thinking will come true. This is because when you think a certain way, you tend to behave in a certain way that, in some way, supports that thinking style.

Believing that nothing good can happen for you will make you stop trying. You will assume that no matter what you do, you will be defeated and cease to look for possible solutions to make your life better. You will lack motivation. By not going after what you want, you attract feelings of emptiness and unfulfillment. Going through life from a place of misery only attracts more misery. You know what they say - misery loves company. When you are thinking negatively, you behave negatively which results in you doing things that prevent you from welcoming good things into your life. Whether it is avoiding situations, engaging in conflict, being unmotivated, or acting in ways that align with a negative attitude, it will attract more negativity and lack into your life. If you are not in a good place in your life right now, being open to change and good opportunities (in whatever form they may take place and whatever time they may come) will still help you feel more hopeful about your life than being closed off due to your negative thoughts. By thinking negatively, you are shutting the door to potential happiness that could come knocking.

Think of a time when you were having negative thoughts and that brought more negativity into your life. Write down what happened.

_____
_____
_____
_____
_____

How did you cope with it?

_____
_____
_____
_____
_____

Now, take some time to introspect a bit. Think back to specific moments in your life that can help guide you in figuring out how you think and behave. You may not get the answer immediately, which is why deep introspection is needed (with practice, you will learn how to be more self-aware and reflect). Take your time and be brutally honest with your answers: this is a no judgment zone and you will only gain from this workbook if you identify your pain points, so that you can work on them.

What kinds of negative thoughts do you usually get? What are they usually about? Write them down.

_____
_____
_____
_____
_____
_____
_____

Identify the specific triggers that instigate your negative thought spiral:

_____
_____
_____
_____
_____
_____
_____
_____

Where does your mind usually go when an intrusive thought enters your mind?

___

___

___

___

___

___

How do you feel when you get stuck on a negative thought?

___

___

___

___

___

___

___

How do your negative thoughts impact your daily life?

_____
_____
_____
_____
_____
_____

When you are thinking negatively, what kinds of words do you use in your sentences when you speak to people?

_____
_____
_____
_____
_____
_____

CHAPTER 2:
IDENTIFY YOUR STRUGGLES

Similar to the previous chapter, this chapter focuses on building the skill of self-awareness. Only when you are truly aware of who you are can you move forward to make changes and grow. Of course, it is easy to say, "reflect and identify your struggles", because many times our conscious mind might not be aware of what we unconsciously struggle with, which makes it difficult for us to recognize our vulnerabilities. When we actually sit down and take the time to identify the areas of our life in which we are not happy, it can feel immensely overwhelming because all of our negative thoughts and emotions might come flooding in at once. On the other hand, you might have the opposite reaction and feel as though your mind has gone completely blank. This usually happens when your conscious mind is not aware of your internal wounds, and so when it comes time to reflect, it can feel like you are grasping at straws.

Although there is no "right way" of self-reflecting, there are a few steps you can take to help nudge yourself in the right direction. Being introspective takes practice: it is like a muscle you need to keep exercising in order to build. The more you exercise it, the stronger it gets. A pessimistic or unhopeful mindset is usually the manifestation of inner wounds that are yet to be healed.

You may try to bury the wounds you have from the past as deeply as you can; however, the mind almost always has a way of making those scars manifest in other ways, and negative thinking is one of them. Unfortunately, you sometimes might not even know that the way you look at the world is a result of unprocessed emotions, or maybe even trauma, and your perception of life is just the tip of the iceberg.

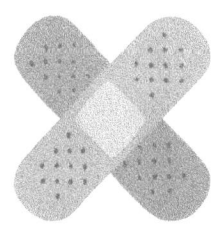

The rest of your scars are hidden below the surface, in your unconscious mind, and sometimes it takes some deep digging to reveal them.
Self-reflection may seem scary; after all, you are uncovering some painful parts of your life and experiencing uncomfortable emotions and thoughts when doing this. It is part of the process. Although it seems like a mammoth task that would drain the life out of you, it can actually be very enlightening and relieving.

You may think that in order to be a strong woman, you need to suppress the pain you might have, put on a brave face for the world, and just hustle on. While that does show motivation, it can be detrimental for your mental health because even though you are trying to move forward, your mind needs your attention.

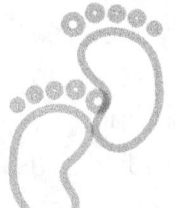
Think of your mind as a newborn baby. When a newborn baby needs your attention, they cry out for help to alert you that they either need to be fed, burped, or changed. You immediately tend to the baby and give them what they need, resulting in them feeling great again and ready to take on the world.

Think of your mind as a newborn baby. When a newborn baby needs your attention, they cry out for help to alert you that they either need to be fed, burped, or changed. You immediately tend to the baby and give them what they need, resulting in them feeling great again and ready to take on the world. Your mind is no different; it will alert you that you need to give attention to your emotional scars and heal them for your mind to be at peace. Instead of screaming at the top of its lungs, your mind could instead present you with intrusive thoughts, flashbacks, uncomfortable emotions, anxiety or another form of alert to let you know that you need to focus on giving yourself the attention and care you need to feel better again. As negative thoughts are usually a manifestation of something deeper, you need to dig deep.

How do we reveal the rest of the iceberg? You start by labeling each intrusive thought that pops into your head, especially if they are recurrent. For example, if you struggle with feelings of inadequacy in a relationship and you get a thought that says something like, "I am not good enough for my partner", you can label it as "the inadequacy thought".

Labeling your thoughts adds some distance between you and that thought so that you can look at it objectively and see it for what it truly is - just a few words that your mind has conjured up that hold no value until you place value on it.

Thus, the next time you get a thought surrounding feeling inadequate, instead of jumping down the negative thought spiral, you can say to yourself, "oh look, the inadequate thought is here again". You are treating the thought as an intrusive guest in your house and simply allowing it to pass you by. We will dive deeper into how to allow thoughts to pass by in the upcoming chapters, for now just remember that not every thought needs to be held on to and that you can simply label them so that you know what they entail without having to go down that rabbit hole.

You can do the same for uncomfortable emotions. If you are feeling overwhelmed or have a negative feeling within you, try to label the emotion. Is it sadness? Is it guilt? Is it anger? Is it anxiety? Labeling your emotions also allows you to know how you are feeling and almost observe it from a distance like a scientist. Simply saying "I am feeling anxious now" can put your mind at ease knowing that you are aware of how you are feeling and are not struggling to identify what is going on inside of you.

Once you have labeled your thoughts and emotions, ask yourself what is causing you to think this thought or feel this emotion. Many times, something has triggered it to happen. It could be an event, another thought, a person, a memory, a physical act or something else. Try to trace back to what was happening before you got this thought or emotion. If there was nothing specific that happened or many triggers could have caused this, break it down and think about each one individually to see if it fits the thought or the emotion. Here is where your scientist brain comes into the picture and analyzes what might have caused a reaction in your mind and body. Finding a causal link to the intrusive thought or emotion can help shed light onto what surface-level triggers you are most vulnerable to.

After identifying the trigger (or triggers), this is where the digging comes in. You need to be the archaeologist of your own mind and excavate the root causes of your triggers. Ask yourself, "why do these particular triggers bother me?" and see what answers your mind presents you with.

If you are just starting to introspect, maybe do this in a safe space where there is minimal distraction and you can truly be vulnerable with yourself. Maybe you curl up on the couch in the living room or sit in your favorite spot in your lawn or on your balcony with a hot cup of tea so that you can take that time to focus your attention on the deep waters of your psyche.

If you want to do this in an environment outside your home, you could even consider doing this at the beach or at the peak of a hill after a good hike. The point is to start your journey of self-reflection in a place where you feel most relaxed and at peace, so that you can give this process your full attention without feeling threatened by external distractions or possible anxiety.

When you ask yourself why you are feeling or thinking a certain way, more often than not there will be an answer. Even if it is the most surface-level or basic answer, it still gives you a good starting point. From thereon, you use this as your first clue for your investigation to uncover the truth about the root cause of this trigger. This first clue will lead you to the next clue about why you feel or think a certain way; and in this manner, keep asking yourself what causes that clue until you are unable to uncover any more clues. This will be your final answer.

In some cases, you might feel stuck and not be able to come up with an answer because the answer might be hiding deep within you, and that is completely okay. Do not be too hard on yourself. This journey of self-reflection does not happen overnight; everybody has their own timeline of self-discovery and sometimes it can take a really long time for you to learn things about yourself. You usually get your answers when you are in a peaceful environment or you can even get your answers when you start to do things for yourself that make you genuinely happy.

When you connect with yourself through hobbies, genuine people, meditation and other things that bring your soul joy, you feed yourself with positivity and you begin to uncover many truths about who you are, which include the emotional turmoil you have been through and how those have shaped you to be the person you are today. It is possible to be your own therapist and ask yourself why you feel and think certain things; the trick is to be authentically curious about yourself and keep an open mind about the possible truths you may uncover.

Only when you are honest with yourself can you truly know what emotional wounds you might be carrying.

Try a practice round now. Remember to breathe through all the difficult emotions you may face through this process and soothe yourself so that you have the courage and motivation to keep going:

If you are going through something right now or were going through something recently, try labeling the thoughts you were getting. What are the labels of the intrusive thoughts you have/had?

_____

_____

_____

_____

_____

Label the emotions you feel/felt surrounding these thoughts:

_____

_____

_____

_____

_____

What was the trigger that caused these thoughts and emotions to pop up?

_____

_____

_____

_____

_____

Why do you think this trigger bothered you? This will be your first clue to uncovering the truth about your emotional wound.

_____

_____

_____

_____

_____

_____

Why do you think the first clue bothered you so much? This will be your second clue.

_____

_____

_____

_____

_____

_____

Why do you think this trigger bothered you? This will be your first clue to uncovering the truth about your emotional wound.

___

___

___

___

___

___

Why do you think the first clue bothered you so much? This will be your second clue.

___

___

___

___

___

___

Try uncovering your next few clues (take as many clues as you need) based on what you have found in the first 2 clues: ✒

_____

_____

_____

_____

_____

Have you come to a revelation? If so, what do you think the root cause is for this intrusive thought? ✒

_____

_____

_____

_____

_____

If you have not yet had your eureka moment, do not fret. You will get there. The important thing is to at least start the process and get the hang of looking within yourself and unpacking so that you can take a step closer towards healing.

PART 2
ADOPTING A POSITIVE MINDSET

CHAPTER 3:
PRACTICING GRATITUDE

What does it mean to be grateful? Practicing gratitude entails being thankful for aspects of your life as they are or were. This means you would be thankful for whatever you have in your life, regardless of what you think you might be lacking, and see the positivity of having your life come together the way it has today. You might think you know how to be grateful, however, believe it or not, there is more to it than just saying "thank you".

Being truly grateful is an art you need to practice and if you do not do it enough now, chances are that you are not aware of how to be grateful in a way that makes you see how great your life is at this moment. If you are reading this workbook hoping to change your mindset to a positive one, then it is likely that you struggle with practicing gratitude and you need to learn how to adopt this habit into your daily life.

Being thankful for the things you have or have had in your life is important for your mental wellbeing because it opens your eyes and makes you see that your life is not all that bad. No matter what you may be going through, gratitude helps you realize that there is a reason to get up in the morning and that there is something that will keep you going. There are several benefits to practicing gratitude; and if you build this habit every day, you will start to see your outlook turn into a positive one. So, what are some of the benefits of regularly practicing gratitude?

Physical health improves

Practicing gratitude improves physical wellbeing. Studies show that increased gratitude in one's life has a correlational effect on their sleeping patterns, immunity, blood pressure, and even any aches and pains they might be experiencing! Recognizing the good in your life decreases the chances of staying up at night and worrying about what you do not have. You start to feel better about your life and do not spend as much time focusing on the negatives as you otherwise would.

Your mind finds some peace and is able to relax better when it comes time to turn out the lights for bed. Being grateful also means being less stressed; therefore, your blood pressure decreases because you are not constantly anxious. Your immunity also gets stronger because you feel happier than you would have if you were thinking negatively and unable to see the blessings in your life. Your mental health has a direct impact on your physical health; so if you are working on your mental wellbeing, there is a huge chance that your physical wellbeing will improve drastically too.

Strengthens interpersonal relationships

Gratitude allows you to build connections and maintain them better too. When we meet someone new and we are getting to know them, it is easy to nitpick at their flaws and think about all the reasons why we should not be associated with this particular person. In fact, sometimes people only recognize other people's weaknesses which clouds their judgment of who the person really is. This is unfortunate because everybody is human, everybody has their flaws.

Nobody is perfect. Someone who has a negative mindset will most likely focus on people's imperfect traits and think of those traits as "bad traits" when in actuality, they are just a part of who the person is and should be accepted. By practicing gratitude, you start to accept people for who they truly are (with the "good" and the "bad") and not hold their weaknesses against them. You will simply acknowledge the person as they are as a whole and embrace all their traits to form a more informed opinion of them. Of course, if you really do not get along with someone, then it is not mandatory for you to maintain a bond with them. You do not need to keep every single person you meet in your close circles; however, for the ones who are important to you, it is better to recognize their good traits and applaud them for their growth as you keep on getting to know them. Being grateful for other people allows you to appreciate your support system and can give you reassurance that you are not alone in this world. You have people in your corner who will be there for you and simply make your life worth living. When you are thankful for the people you have in your life, you tend to put more effort into maintaining the relationship, which the other person will appreciate as well.

Your relationships will seem more authentic and will bring you true joy. Social relationships are important for humanity's survival and should be nurtured in order to grow. This means appreciating the person for everything they bring into your life because chances are they are in your life for a reason. Expressing gratitude to the other person also makes them feel seen, which makes them want to be closer to you too. Gratitude brings along with it an array of positive emotions and being appreciated is a surefire way for a bond to strengthen and deepen.

Increases happiness

When you reflect on a good part of your life, you tend (even for a moment) to relive that aspect of your life in your mind and acknowledge that it is something that brings positivity. Instead of believing the grass is always green on the other side, you start to focus on taking care of your own garden. Gratitude opens up your heart to see the good things and people in your life and, as a result, you tend to feel more satisfied with your life.

Greater life satisfaction leads to increased happiness because you experience positive emotions and your thoughts start to have positive words in them. Instead of having words like "do not have" or "cannot do" or "will not happen" in your thoughts, you start to have words like "it is possible" and "can do" and "will happen" instead. The way you speak to yourself changes because the same things that were present in your life now seem much more abundant, and you start to tell yourself optimistic things because you can recognize how much you actually already have. Overall, giving thanks makes you happier and can show you how amazing life can truly be.

Reduces the intensity of mental illnesses
Mental illnesses, depending upon which type is prevalent in your life (if any), have a way of making your life feel unfulfilling and sometimes even painful to live. It can be tough to see outside of the pain your mind is experiencing, which is understandable. After all, mental illnesses are beasts of their own that bully your mind into believing that life usually only brings negativity, when in reality this is not the case.

When you are struggling with mental illness, it can be extremely difficult to practice gratitude since you are allocating most of your energy into simply surviving through the day and trying to stay afloat without drowning. Your mind gets so mentally exhausted that sometimes it is unable to see pockets of light that might shine through those dark and ominous clouds. However, practicing gratitude while suffering from mental illness is an effective way to reduce the burden that comes with that illness. It might sound almost impossible to do, but counting your blessings, however miniscule they may seem to you, can lower the intensity of many mental illnesses. By seeing that there is some good in your life, you feel more hopeful that the glass is half full and not half empty. There is evidence to show that there are aspects of your life that are worth smiling about and can help pull you through even the darkest days. Since being grateful increases happiness, life satisfaction and gives you hope, your mind creates space for positive thoughts and emotions by overriding some of the negative or worrisome thoughts you would originally have, resulting in you being able to better cope with mental illness too.

You feel more hopeful
Being grateful for your life and the opportunities and the people in it gives you hope for the future. You have a sense of reassurance that things might not be so bad because there is already existing proof in your life that highlights the great things you have. Instead of hoping from a place of emptiness, you are hoping for things from a place of abundance. By appreciating what you already have, you put yourself in a more positive space and the universe can sense the positive energy you are exerting. As a result, you attract more positivity into your life as well. Even if things are looking a little bleak now, gratitude allows you to recognize even the smallest wins and hope for more to come in the future. With hope, you are able to heal your wounds and get through each day knowing that life is actually worth living.

Boosts your self-esteem

When you acknowledge and give thanks for what you have in your life right now, you realize just how much is being done for you by yourself, other people and the universe. The fact that all of these wonderful things in your life have manifested brings to light just how valuable you are. Sometimes, when we think negatively, it is easy to have thoughts that make you believe that you are not important in the world and your needs do not matter. This negative inner dialogue tends to push your self-esteem down and you end up having a low sense of self-worth.

If you are familiar with the feeling of having low self-esteem, you are also familiar with the negative thoughts you have surrounding how life will never work out the way you want it to. You probably spend a lot of your time identifying things that are missing in your life and as a result, you believe that you might not deserve good things. Unfortunately, your mind makes you behave in ways that are consistent with your thoughts, so if your thoughts are telling you that you are not worthy of being happy and that no good things will come by, then chances are you will behave in ways that will only reinforce that and solidify the false notion that you do not deserve to be happy.

Practicing gratitude is an effective exercise that reveals how many great things and people you currently have in your life, which will give you the confidence to know that you also are valuable. Your attention starts to shift away from what you wish you had in the future to what you currently have in the present. Being grateful for the present boosts self-esteem because you see the good parts of your life; this reassures you that you do deserve good things and they are attainable for you as well - the present moment proves that.

Makes you more selfless

Counting your blessings and giving thanks, no matter what form they come in - whether they manifest in the form of opportunities, cash, people, food, material items or anything else - makes you realize just how good you might already have it. You start to want to give back to the world because you may recognize that there are some people out there who might not be fortunate enough to have what you already have. It is so easy to get lost in thought about the one or two things that are lacking, however it is also just as easy to get lost in gratitude about all the things that you do have and how those are making your life easier and happier.

It is said that selfless acts bring lasting happiness, and when you act selflessly from a place of gratitude, you are likely to make yourself as well as other people feel genuinely happy in the long-run. You become more compassionate towards other people, as well as to yourself. Embodying positivity through gratitude makes you want to make other people feel the same way as well, and so you perform selfless acts that would help someone else feel as though life can be great for them too.

For example, when you express gratitude for having wonderful people in your life who care about you, you start to appreciate those bonds much more deeply. As a result, you may want to volunteer at a nursing home to spend time with elderly people who might not have many friends or family they can count on during their daily lives. In this instance, you would want to be the bond they can count on. Giving thanks for what your life has presented you with makes you think less about gaining for yourself and instead makes you want to give more to other people.

If you are unsure about how to start practicing gratitude, that is okay. There is no "correct way" to give thanks; the main point is to acknowledge what you already have and say thank you in whatever form you feel most comfortable. Here are some suggestions to get you started:

Start with acknowledging just one thing that has made you happy each day

Start small. At the end of each day, reflect on the happenings of the day and think of one moment that made you happy. If it was a particular difficult day, then think of something that helped make a moment in the day slightly more bearable for you.

The goal of this exercise is to make you practice seeing that even the worst days do have a glimmer of light hidden somewhere in them, you just need to acknowledge it and appreciate it.

It could be something as simple as "I am grateful for being able to have taken a relaxing hot shower today" or something as deep as "I am grateful that I was able to go to work and earn some money today". What you feel grateful for will vary day over day, so be sure to take each day as it comes and identify one thing for that day in particular that made you feel lighter.

You can write these in a gratitude list or you can simply say what you are grateful for out loud or in your head before you drift off to sleep. Doing this at night ends your day on a more positive note because no matter how horrible your day might have been, reiterating one thing that made it less horrible for even a moment can remind you that there are things to be thankful for and happy about. As you keep practicing this exercise, your mind will start to recognize more things to be grateful about each day.

From 1 thing per day you can increase it to 3 things you are grateful for each day. Of course, some of these will repeat as you permanently instill this practice into your daily life, and that is normal. The goal is to keep doing this everyday so that you can adopt a more positive outlook on your life.

Try doing this now. List 3 things that are grateful for today:

_____

_____

_____

_____

Recognize the lessons you learned during the tough times

Life is not a walk in the park. There will be times when you feel completely lost and wonder why certain events are happening to you. The classic "why me?" is something that crosses all of our minds at some point in our lives and it is only natural to fall down the pit of despair when we are going through trying times. During those times, you may feel that there is no sunshine through all of those dark and gloomy clouds. When it rains it pours, and there is no shade for you to protect yourself against the flood of stress that might come with the storm.

Though it is completely natural to feel overwhelmed during stressful periods in your life, it is important to note that you have the power to decide how you want to react to those situations. You can assume that you need to surrender to every single negative thought and emotion you experience during the hard moments, or you can realize that difficult times bring with them important lessons for you to learn in order to grow and lead a fulfilling life.

It might be hard to be grateful for the trying times when you are currently going through them, but it gets easier to appreciate the lesson you learned by going through that time in hindsight. Think back to the times when you felt as though you were struggling to keep your head above the water. Reflect on the emotions and the thoughts you had during those times and what you would go through every single day.

Doing this may bring back some painful memories, so the first thing to be thankful for is the strength you had to get through that time and be where you are today. You are still alive and you are still breathing - you made it. Show gratitude to the universe for giving you the ability to trek through that rocky period. Recognizing your strength then leads you to reflect on what else you learned through that rough period, because chances are lessons from the tough times shaped you to be the person you are today.

More often than not, even the darkest of times taught you something and have made you a more resilient person. Being grateful for the lessons you have learned and who you have become as a result of those stressful times will give you the confidence to know that you can get through anything in life and come out the other side as a stronger person.

Reflect on one difficult period in your life. What were you going through at the time?

_____

_____

_____

_____

How did you cope at that time?

_____

_____

_____

_____

What lessons do you think you learned from that time?

_____

_____

_____

_____

_____

_____

Write down 3 statements about that time to express gratitude for the lessons you learned. These statements can start with "I am grateful...":

_____

_____

_____

_____

_____

_____

Maintain a gratitude journal

The best way to motivate yourself to practice gratitude is to maintain a gratitude journal. It is a more tangible way to reflect on the good parts of your life because writing down things you are grateful for in a journal makes it feel more real. When you are thinking back to things that you are grateful for; although you are recounting things that are real, your mind is focusing on a thought which is intangible. It can be hard to truly feel grateful sometimes for something that has popped up in a thought, but when you write it down, you actually see the words on a piece of paper. The words that were in your head have come alive on paper; the good things in your life have come alive on that piece of paper. You know what they say: seeing is believing; and when you see the words outlining all the great things you have going for you, you start to truly believe that your life is wonderful.

If you are not sure about how to start, there are various awesome gratitude journals online you can buy. You could even look for gratitude journal templates and try to create your own if you are feeling creative! It could be a fun activity for you to do that makes you happy and the activity of making the journal might even make it onto your gratitude list! Personalize your gratitude journal so it feels more like you and like home. The pages of your gratitude journal should invite you to pour positivity onto them, so use your creative freedom to make those pages mirror your soul.

There are a variety of gratitude journal formats out there, and you can choose which one resonates with you most. Some of them include sections such as:

- Things I am grateful for today
- Gratitude mantra
- People I am grateful for
- Things I have learned
- Today I will…

…and so on and so forth. Decide which template you would like to use for yourself and start writing!

Let us have some creative fun and get in touch with the little girl inside of you. If you have or had a gratitude journal, how would you personalize it to make it feel positive? Think about colors, fonts, stickers, etc.

Reduce the amount you complain

This might sound harsh, but if you tend to complain a lot, then you are probably preventing yourself from thinking positively. Venting about your life is one thing; in fact, it is encouraged because bottling up your emotions can be detrimental to your mental health. Expressing how you feel, in whatever form you are comfortable with, can make you feel as though you have lifted a heavy weight from your chest and can breathe easier.

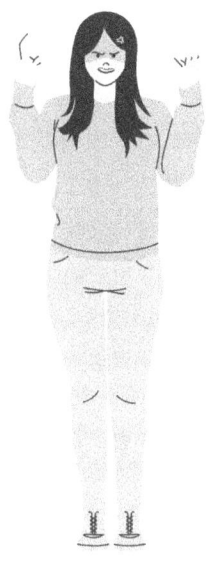

Emotional expression is a good thing. However, complaining is when you cross the border into constantly expressing your dissatisfaction with something, even if it might not be a big deal. For example, if you had a long day at work because you needed to submit a deliverable by a certain deadline, you would probably feel exhausted by the time you came home. Emotional expression would have you say that you feel burnt out and that you felt like you were under a tremendous amount of pressure to get this done on time. That is a healthy way to express how the event made you feel.

However, if you were to complain, you would probably say something along the lines of "I had to work so late today, what is the point of even having this job?". In this instance, you are expressing your annoyance for the situation, but you are complaining about something that was likely a one-off event and was also likely important to do and part of your job description.

By questioning the point of even having the job, you are doing the opposite of being grateful - you are telling the universe that you do not appreciate this job and that it adds no value to your life, because of this one single event. To complain is to disregard the positives of the situation because of one negative aspect and solely focus on that negative aspect.

Complaining is a form of expression that makes you see life through tunnel vision. Complaining about cold food at a restaurant is acceptable because you have the right to let them know that you expected to pay for a hot meal. However, complaining in this context has more to do with when something in your life is not going your way and you think complaining is the only way to change it.

People often complain when they think there is no way out of their situation; however, this is only a result of their negative mindset. It is imperative to realize that you have control over your life. If something is not going your way, think of an alternative solution. Of course, you can feel extremely disappointed if something does not go according to plan, however, do not sing the same tune over and over again. Instead, think of what else you can do to add just as much happiness to your life in some other way if something did not go as planned.

Complaining puts our negative energy into the world, and it is more likely o attract more negative energy back to you. Instead, try to fix the problem or find an alternative and say to yourself that even though things did not go as planned, things will still be okay. You will survive and make the best out of whatever the alternative solution is.

When you reduce the amount you complain, you start to become grateful for everything you do have. Every person's life has negatives and positives in it; however, complaining only makes you focus on the aspects that are dissatisfactory to you. Decreasing the amount you complain helps you focus less on the negatives and shifts your attention to the positives. Before you know it, you see how abundant your life truly is and you start to feel grateful for all the things that make your life worth living.

What are some things you often complain about?

_____

_____

_____

_____

_____

Now, rewrite those complaints to put a positive spin on each of them:

_____

_____

_____

_____

_____

Do some volunteer work and give back to the community

A wonderful way of practicing gratitude is to give back to the community. You could make generous donations to charities that you support; that would definitely be a great way to practice gratitude. However, it has been shown that engaging in volunteer work can increase levels of gratitude and fulfilment in most people. Human beings are social animals and we rely on each other in order to survive and thrive. When you do something for someone else through volunteer work, you are interacting with them on a more personal level and this puts things into perspective for you. This is not to say that you can only realize what you have when you see what others do not have, but it does sometimes shine some light on the blessings that you are unfortunate to have that other people are not as lucky to have.

When you help someone out, it also makes you realize the time and effort it takes for someone to help you. You might not always recognize just how much someone might have done for you to make your life just a little bit easier, so volunteering is a way to be thankful for everything that people have done for you over the course of your life, no matter how big or small the gesture of kindness is.

Volunteering makes you appreciate the people in your life and want to pay that kindness forward - it is a cycle of gratitude and selflessness. You feel as though you are part of something bigger than yourself and your life starts to fill up with more meaning. Doing things for someone other than yourself gives you purpose, and it is only natural to start feeling grateful for the opportunity to be able to help other people. That sense of community you build through volunteering opens up your heart to more kindness, fulfilment and gratitude.

What kind of volunteer work would you like to do?

_____

_____

_____

_____

How often would you like to do it?

_____

_____

_____

_____

_____

What first step can you take to start volunteering and giving back to the community?

_____

_____

_____

_____

_____

_____

Do some gratitude rituals

Here is where your fun and creative side comes into play! You can think of some gratitude rituals you would like to incorporate into your life that you think will make this habit more engaging, so that you feel excited to give thanks. The best part about this is that you get to decide what the ritual is, how often you want to do it, and what constitutes its success. You could simply recount your day before going to bed and list 3 things you felt grateful for in your head; but why not make it a little more fun and engage in some ritualistic activity to really get your gratitude juices flowing.

When people perform rituals, it is usually because they have desires they want met, and they hope these rituals will bring those desires closer to their grasp. This concept can be used for gratitude, as you would be performing these rituals to bring your desire to be more grateful to fruition. Performing rituals can also strengthen the skill of discipline, as it becomes a habit and you feel motivated to maintain the frequency of doing it too.

A ritual can make you feel emotionally stable because you are doing something for yourself in order to feel as though you have control over the outcomes in your life. By maintaining a ritual, you could in fact be pulling the outcome you desire closer to you, as you would be performing acts that align with what you want. Similarly, performing gratitude rituals can pull your desire to think positively closer to you because you are habitually doing small things to manifest that positive outcome for yourself.

You have all the freedom to decide what your rituals can be, but here are some suggestions in case you are having trouble figuring it out:

Write thank you notes

You could decide to write thank you notes at the end of every week to thank the universe for all the amazing things that had happened to you that week. It does not necessarily only have to be for a person; it can be addressed to your bathtub for providing you with such a comfortable space to soak all your stress away. It could be addressed to the appliances in your kitchen for helping you cook that delicious meal you had been craving for days. It could even be addressed to the universe in general, or whatever energy you believe in, to thank the universal energy for providing you with an income to survive on or for providing you with great people in your life on whom you can rely. The point is to shift the focus outwards and look outside of yourself to express gratitude for everything you have.

To:

_____

_____

_____

To:

_____

_____

_____

To:

_____

_____

_____

Fill up a jar with gratitude notes

Filling a jar with gratitude notes is a wonderful way to look back at everything you have felt grateful for and to remind yourself of how blessed you are. Having a cute little jar with notes stating what you are thankful for sitting on your bedside table or on your desk can also serve as an adorable reminder to always be grateful. Sometimes the struggles of life can bring us down and we might forget to cherish its good moments. This jar will be a physical reminder that life is not all bad. Plus, it is not a bad decorative piece for your side table or desk!

You could do one note every week for a year and then look through all your notes at the end of the year to reflect back on the positives of that year. The New Year can be an emotional time and if you are the type of person who focuses on only the pain points of that year, then this ritual might be a good one for you to try. It will be an amazing revelation at the end of the year that will show you not only the things you can be grateful about, but also show you that you in fact WERE grateful for these things at one point in your life and that it is possible to capture that positive feeling again.

Have some fun with this! Try planning what your gratitude jar will look like.

What color would you want your jar to be?

_____

_____

_____

_____

What color notes would you want to put in the jar?

_____
_____
_____

Are there any other decorative elements you would like to adorn your jar with? (Lights, stickers, etc.)

_____
_____
_____

How often would you want to put a note in your gratitude jar?

_____
_____
_____

If you were to put a gratitude note in a jar for this week, what would you put as your first one?

_____
_____
_____

Reward yourself as a thank you

Being grateful for what the world has given you is a wonderful way to connect with what is outside of you to remind yourself that there are external forces at play that can help you get what you need or want. Being grateful for everything around you also keeps you grounded and anchored in a positive reality, showing you that the world is not such a bad place. Emitting vibes of gratitude outwards makes you feel reassured that the world is on your side and that everything will be okay.

While it is a beautiful act to express gratitude outwardly, it is just as beautiful to be grateful for the things you do for yourself. The person you spend the most amount of time with on a daily basis is you, and so you need to treat yourself right. You need to be doing things for yourself that make your life easier and more fulfilling.

Unfortunately, it is human nature to look for validation and care from external sources, after all who does not want to feel loved and cared for? However, we often forget that the most important kind of love and validation is the type we give to ourselves because that is ultimately what shapes us to be who we are in the current moment. As a result, we take ourselves for granted and do not think about thanking ourselves.

Life can get pretty challenging, whether you are drowning in work or tied up with family responsibilities, and it is difficult to spend time with yourself. However, even the little things that you do end up doing for yourself, such as buying yourself a cup of coffee on the way to work or remembering to fold your laundry so your clothes do not stack up on your bed, are acts of self-care.

Just because you are performing these acts of self-care for yourself does not mean that these acts are unimportant - they make your life a little easier and a little better, so be sure to thank yourself for doing them. Expressing gratitude to yourself for all the things you do for yourself will increase your self-esteem because you are showing yourself respect and appreciation by thanking yourself.

You are recognizing all you do and are amazed by the effort and time you put in just to make things a little more bearable. If you can express gratitude to other people, other things, and to the universe, why not give thanks to yourself? You are also an important person and deserve to be appreciated by the person who relies on you the most: yourself.

You could simply say "thank you" to yourself, but that can get monotonous, so sometimes try rewarding yourself to express gratitude. For example, if you are a mother and have managed to put your kids to bed early, thank yourself for doing this by putting on a rose face mask and reading that book you have not gotten a chance to read until now. That would be a wholesome way to reward yourself for doing something to make your life a little easier. You do not always have to reward yourself for every little thing that you do, but make it a habit to recognize all that you do and treat yourself for it as a thank you.

In what ways can you thank yourself for all that you do? Write down some ways:

_____

_____

_____

_____

_____

_____

_____

What do you do for yourself to make your life easier?

___

___

___

___

___

___

How will you thank yourself for reading this book?

___

___

___

___

___

___

Share your gratitude with your friends and family

It is common practice to express gratitude if someone does something for you or says something wonderful to you. Saying thank you is a social construct that has helped deepen bonds between people for generations. We usually express gratitude when someone gives us a gift or when they say we look stunning today; those are excellent reasons to thank them. However, sometimes we might miss thanking them for other things they may do for us that may not be as obvious.

Sometimes it is easy to take other people for granted if they are extremely close to you. For example, if your sibling comes to your apartment to eat a meal with you and washes the dishes because they can see you are tired, that is also a great reason to express gratitude. Although they are your family and you did not ask them to help you out, they doing so themselves shows that they spent their energy to make your life easier.

For this, expressing gratitude makes them feel appreciated and loved too. You can express your gratitude to them in whatever form you feel most comfortable: you can verbalize it, give them hugs, throw a dinner party, write them a letter or send them a sweet video message. Do whatever you feel is best for you to genuinely express your love and gratitude for the person - whatever you do, they will truly appreciate it.

You could also share your gratitude with other people. This means that if you are grateful for the way your life turned out, even if they had nothing to do with it, you can share your happiness and gratitude with the people around you. When you are genuinely appreciative of the little things in your life, you exude positive vibes. In fact, your positivity will encourage other people to start being more grateful for their lives as well and motivate them to do more things for themselves. Every person's life has two sides to it - the side that is challenging and the side that is going well for them. Criticizing your life brings you no benefits, so you might as well share with people everything you are grateful for so that they can also participate in your positivity for you and for themselves. Trust me, it works.

Which people in your life help make your life easier and better? Why?

_____

_____

_____

How would you express your gratitude to these people?

_____

_____

_____

What are some things in your life you feel grateful for that you would want to share with your friends and family?

_____

_____

_____

Stay present in the current moment

One of the best ways to practice gratitude is to be present. Many times, we are so bothered by what has happened in the past or so worried about what might happen in the future that we ruin the present. We miss out on life's wonderful moments today because we are so consumed by our yesterdays and our tomorrows. It is human tendency to ruminate on issues; we are a species that likes to problem-solve and take control of our lives. However, there needs to be a balance between healthy rumination and obsessing over things that are not important in the present moment.

When the mind is constantly occupied with negativity, we are snatching away the precious moments we could use today to make our lives great. You have been given a life and you have the power to write your story at every moment, and neglecting that story to think about past or future stories is the opposite of practicing gratitude.

Imagine yourself at the beach. You can smell the salt in the air and can feel the cool breeze in your face. You can hear the waves crashing and can feel your feet sinking into the warm dry sand. It is a moment in which you need to be fully aware so that you can cherish it. In order to be able to do this, you need to bring yourself back to the present and focus your attention on what is in front of you.

When you give your mind a break from thinking about everything that could go wrong and simply live in the moment, you will feel lighter. Most of the time, the struggles you are trying to overcome are caused by negative thoughts. If you gave your mind a rest from these thoughts and simply stayed present in the moment, you would realize that you will be okay. You will survive whatever it is that is troubling you and in fact, you will feel thankful for having the chance to be at the beach and experience all of these sensory delights.

Being in the moment gives you the opportunity to soak in whatever is going on around you and will trigger a positive reaction in your mind that will make you feel grateful for the moment. Staying present is a beautiful way of giving thanks to the universe for all it has given you.

When was the last time you were fully present in a beautiful moment?

_____

_____

_____

_____

_____

_____

_____

_____

Practicing gratitude through these techniques, and any more that you can think of, allows you to replace the negative associations you have with life with positive feelings instead. What can be better than that?

CHAPTER 4:
BUILD SELF-ESTEEM

What exactly is self-esteem? Self-esteem is how much you determine yourself worthy of love and respect and how confident you are about your abilities. Every person in the world has a certain level of self-esteem at any given moment - it is a part of your personality that does not ever go away, it just changes over time. Someone might have very high self-esteem whereby they think very highly of themselves and can sometimes come across as egoistic and entitled.

Another person might have very low self-esteem and not deem themselves worthy of good things and so they come across as having low confidence and being complacent. People fall on different points on the self-esteem spectrum; while it is important to build your self-esteem, it is just as important to not allow yourself to cross the line into arrogance.

A synonym for self-esteem is also self-worth, which is ultimately what you are measuring when we talk about self-esteem. How worthy do you think you are of good things? This basically means how worthy you think you are of love, financial stability, career progression, strong friendships, etc. If you have high self-esteem, you know you are worthy of all the good things, which is a great mental space to be in!

However, arrogance and entitlement comes into play when someone with high self-esteem is unable to accept when sometimes things do not go their way and they lash out because they believe they were "wronged" when in actuality it might just be because sometimes life does not go according to plan. Someone who has high self-esteem but is not arrogant will obviously be disappointed that they did not get what they wanted; however, they will also know that they are worthy of many other good things in life and strive to achieve those, while humbly accepting that what they wanted was not meant for them and that it is okay to be accommodating. Having a healthy level of self-esteem means being secure about the things you have as well as the things you do not have, because you know you are worthy no matter what.

If you have low self-esteem, it is very likely that you do not think positively. People who think positively have thoughts that reaffirm their worthiness. If you are struggling to think positively, one of the biggest contributors to it is probably low self-esteem because you do not truly see just how worthy you are of being happy and how amazing you are. Your thoughts make you doubt things in your life and feel as though you are not good enough and that your life is not good enough.

Positive thinking and high self-esteem go hand in hand - one cannot work without the other. When you start to think positively and feel the positivity within you, you start to put yourself in high regard and realize just how awesome you are. When you realize how awesome you are, you end up having more positive thoughts about where your life can take you. It is a never-ending cycle of positivity.

While every human being is unique, levels of self-esteem can manifest differently depending on the person. However, with that being said, there are some common tell-tale signs of someone with low self-esteem:

Believing you are unlovable

One of the most prominent signs that you have low self-esteem is believing that you are not worthy of love. Almost everybody in this world longs for deep and strong bonds that can make them feel supported and happy. Being loved, in particular, is a wonderful feeling that most people crave. As an extremely social species with the ability to experience a wide spectrum of emotions and thoughts, we crave to feel wanted and receive that admiration from people. When you have low self-esteem, your mind tells you that nobody will love you and that it is because you are not worthy of that love.

You see yourself as inferior to other people and you think that someone you might be interested in fancies someone else over you because that person has attributes that are "better than yours" when this is not the case in reality. It does not always have to only relate to romantic relationships; you could feel unworthy of love when it comes to your family and friends too. If you do not see yourself in high regard, chances are you will think that everyone else sees you the same way. As a result, you end up isolating yourself or you start to feel extremely lonely because you preemptively expect that you will not find people who will love you.

Believing you do not deserve good things
Similar to not believing you are worthy of love, you also believe that you are not worthy of good things in life. This could be new clothes, a new apartment, a nice holiday or anything else that you think would be a great part of your life. Having low self-esteem means that you see these good things as unattainable for yourself. For some reason, your mind has convinced you that you do not deserve to have good things happen to you because you are not as "good as other people".

You may admire other people in your life, but you will always compare yourself to them and conclude that they have amazing lives because they are "better than you". Again, this is your mind conjuring up a narrative that is only meant to hurt you. There is no truth to it. You are just as valuable as any other human being on this planet - who is to say that you are not? You are the only person who can make yourself feel inferior, and this happens when you have low self-esteem.

For example, you might get promoted at work because you have been working yourself to the ground every single day. However, if you have low self-esteem, you will not see this as a win. You will find some tiny flaw within yourself to justify why you do not deserve this good accomplishment. You might not even strive to get things that you want because you might deem yourself to be a failure right from the get go, and so you are stuck in the same place you have been for a while because you are discouraging yourself from going after something good due to a false belief. Having low self-esteem means not being able to see that you are worthy of having good things happen to you just as much as anybody else.

Unable to handle criticism
Since you are already quite fragile because of your low self-esteem, you are unable to handle criticism (even constructive criticism). Facing criticism makes you think that all of those doubts you have had about yourself are true. One tiny remark can make you fall into a spiral of negative emotions. You tend to take feedback quite personally and believe that those remarks are made because you are not worthy. You tie your personality and entire being to that piece of criticism, without realizing that that remark was told about just one specific aspect of yourself.

Having high self-esteem is knowing the areas where you need to grow and that if someone provides you with insight into how you could improve, it is ultimately up to you to believe whether you want to take that advice or not. Being secure within yourself means that even though you might have flaws, you know that you are still a person who is worthy and valuable. You do not let someone pointing out your flaws have the power to make you feel unworthy.

Only you have the power to make yourself feel unworthy ;and if you are unable to handle criticism, chances are you will act emotionally towards the person criticizing you and go down a negative thought spiral later on too. Of course, it is normal to feel upset when someone criticizes you - it is a normal human tendency. However, taking it too emotionally and personally every time is a big sign that you have low self-esteem and cannot handle someone pointing out an attribute you need to work on.

Negative inner dialogue
If you speak to yourself in a discouraging way and mainly have negative thoughts, you likely have very low self-esteem. Believing that you are not worthy is something rooted deep within, due to which your mind throws negative thoughts at you. Since you are not well-versed in standing up for yourself (due to low self-esteem), you believe these thoughts to be true.

For example, you might have gone on a first date with a guy that you were really into. The date went extremely well and you totally hit it off. You would love to go on a second date with him but he has not asked you yet and you do not want to come off sounding too eager either.

Your low self-esteem would be throwing thoughts at you such as "he must not have thought I was pretty enough" or "he probably thought I was boring". These thoughts are just words being thrown around inside your head and these exude negativity. The more you believe these thoughts to be true, the lower your self-esteem drops. Low self-esteem is a beast that throws all of these obnoxious thoughts your way - it is up to you to either hold onto them and believe them to be true, or simply acknowledge that they are trying to bully you and let them go.

Linked to mental illnesses
Low self-esteem has been linked to many mental illnesses, such as anxiety, depression and eating disorders. With anxiety, one's low self-esteem will constantly make them worry about the future and make them believe that whatever comes their way will not be manageable because they "do not have the ability to be strong". Low self-esteem makes them worry about things that might not hold any truth in their life and this causes them to doubt their capability to handle the things that life throws at them, further exacerbating their anxiety.

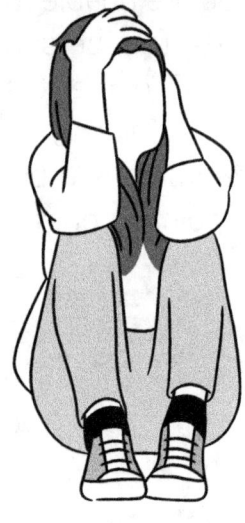

With depression, their low self-esteem makes them believe that they are not good enough and that nothing good will ever happen to them. Low self-esteem strengthens the feeling of hopelessness and as a result, they are unable to console themselves or convince themselves of otherwise. They might not even be able to believe other people when they try to encourage them, because their low self-esteem has convinced them so well that nothing will be good for them. Due to this, their depression becomes painful and they live with it thinking that they are not worthy of love and respect.

Low self-esteem also leads to body image issues, which are the causes of eating disorders amongst many women around the world. Being unable to see how beautiful they really are, due to their low self-esteem, makes them resort to eating habits that would harm them more than help them. Low self-esteem is a bully that can make you fall down an abyss of negativity and if you are suffering from mental illness, low self-esteem can make your mental illness far less manageable too. It is important to build your self-esteem so that you can spare yourself from the mental, emotional and maybe even physical pain you would experience otherwise.

What signs of low self-esteem do you think you exhibit?

_____
_____
_____
_____
_____

What causes low self-esteem?
There is usually a root cause for having low self-esteem; this can vary from person to person. If you think you have low self-esteem, one of the first steps to building your sense of self-worth is digging deep and identifying what might have contributed to your low self-esteem. It could be a combination of reasons, so reflecting on your life can bring to light a lot of information that can help you find out what might be making you feel this way.

① Critical or emotionally absent parents
A lot of the issues embedded in us today stem from our early childhood days; low self-esteem is one of them. As children, we absorb what is happening around us and take it as a source of truth. We are a sponge that is ready to absorb everything that is presented to us, good and bad. The people we crave attention and care from the most are our primary caregivers (usually our parents). The way our parents treat us and raise us, as well as the childhood experiences we have, play a pivotal role in shaping us to be the adults that we are today. Studies show that the type of support children get in the first few years of their life heavily shapes who they become in adulthood, and parents play a huge part of this influence.

If someone has grown up with emotionally supportive parents who catered to their needs growing up and gave them the love they need to feel safe, they most likely grew up to be emotionally healthy adults who recognize their worth. Growing up with parents who used to overly criticize them would make the child believe they are never good enough, which is sadly carried into their adulthood and manifested in other areas of their life. Being raised by emotionally absent parents means the parents were unable to put their child's needs ahead of theirs and so the child was left feeling neglected.

They internalize the notion that their needs are not as important, and so they go about life believing that their needs are not as important as those of other people. The experiences you have in your childhood, particularly with your parents, have a huge effect on your confidence throughout your life.

② Past trauma

Experiencing trauma, in whatever form it manifests, means experiencing a heavily disturbing event or situation that deeply impacts wellbeing. If a person has experienced a traumatic situation in their lives, they would probably struggle to return to normalcy right away, which is completely normal and understandable because your mind and body need time to process whatever has happened and come to terms with it. It can be a grueling process to accept and heal from the trauma, and during this process a person can doubt their ability to get through it. This self-doubt causes their self-esteem to drop drastically and this affects them in other areas of their life.

Whatever your trauma, if you have experienced a trauma that deeply impacted your capabilities to heal and return to normalcy, then chances are your self-esteem has been impacted. The good news is that with determination, therapeutic guidance and emotional support, you can heal from the trauma. When you see yourself become a stronger and more resilient person in your self-healing journey, you feel proud of your growth and start to believe in yourself again, which results in your self-esteem increasing too.

③ Bullying

Being bullied in school is traumatic for a lot of children. Being victim to bullying causes kids and teens to feel unworthy due to the words and actions of their bullies, which sticks with them most of the time unconsciously into adulthood. When bullies call them names, they believe these hurtful words to be true. If they are physically bullied, they take these actions to mean that they are being treated this way due to them not being good enough.

These beliefs are internalized and if they are not resolved, they can be carried into their adult life. Due to the stress experienced from bullying, they are sometimes unable to perform well in other areas in their life such as studying and making friends. They tend to become isolated which can make them feel helpless. They start to think they are meant to be alone and no one will love or want to be friends with them.

Bullying does not always only happen during childhood - it can very much happen in adult life too. It could happen at work, in a relationship or within the family too. Whatever your situation is, if you are a victim of bullying you might find yourself doubting your worthiness of being loved and accepted for who you are, which can have dire consequences on your self-esteem.

④ Struggle with achievement

We face certain tests in life that seem to determine our "worth" - studies, getting a job, getting married and having kids. Sometimes we are pressured to do extremely well in all these areas and accomplish all of them at a certain age. Oftentimes, we compare our achievements to those of others and start to feel inadequate because someone may have accomplished "more" or might have reached their goal earlier than we have.

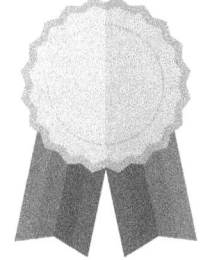

The beast of comparison and feeling inadequate can make us believe that we are not good enough and that whatever we have achieved is minimal because it is not the same accomplishment as someone else's

For children who struggle with getting good grades in school or adults who struggle with achieving work related goals, it can make them feel as though they are not as "smart" as other people, and this severely affects their self-esteem. They internalize this belief and think that they are unworthy of any accomplishments that they do have and constantly think that they will fail in whatever venture they choose to pursue.

5) Past relationships

Unhealthy past relationships can deeply impact our self-esteem. Being in a relationship that was filled with manipulation, betrayal, neglect or any other negative experience can make us feel as though we are the reason we are being treated this way. This is not true at all: the way we are treated in unhealthy relationships is not a reflection of us but a reflection of the other person (unless we are also acting in an equally unhealthy manner too). However, if it is the other person instigating the bad treatment, it is a manifestation of them not being able to heal from their emotional wounds that are unfortunately being projected onto you as their significant other.

As easy as it is to say this although it can be quite difficult to separate ourselves from the reason why we are being treated this way. For example, if you had to face the pain of infidelity in your past relationship, you might have wondered if it was because of something you did (or did not do).

While infidelity is a reflection of the other person's emotional maturity, it is easy to go down a rabbit hole of thinking that maybe it was because of you. However this is not the case and once people realize this, they will start to save their self-esteem.

Being neglected or abused in a past relationship also leaves deep emotional scars that are hard to heal, leaving you thinking that the events that transpired in the relationship might have been because you are unlovable. It is essential to realize that this is not the case: you are extremely loveable and you would add value to anybody's life. The fault lies within the other person who is treating you badly.

Going through painful relationship situations can take a toll on our self-esteem; and if it is not healed, then it can cause deep insecurities within ourselves about how worthy we are of love. If you have been in a painful relationship that questioned your worth, it is very likely that your self-esteem has been deeply impacted and you might still be struggling to believe you will feel loved in a healthy relationship ever again.

Look deep within yourself and take your time to answer these questions. Be honest with yourself.

What do you think is the reason for your low self-esteem? If it is not one of the reasons above, feel free to write down what you think it might be:

_____
_____
_____
_____
_____

What situations in life make you doubt yourself and make your low self-esteem act up?

_____
_____
_____
_____

What specific thoughts do you get that make you question your worth? Write them down here.

_____
_____
_____
_____

Think about one situation that happened in your life in which the thoughts surrounding your low self-esteem caused you to behave in a way that negatively impacted you or someone else. Write down what happened:

_____
_____
_____
_____
_____
_____
_____

Healing and building your self-esteem

Now that you have an idea of your level of self-esteem, where it comes from, and how it usually manifests, you can begin the process of healing. You need to form a positive opinion about yourself because this is the opinion that matters the most. It is the one that decides what your life is going to look like and if it is an unfavorable opinion, your life is not going to look like how you envisioned it. Having low self-esteem is something rooted deep within yourself; however, it is very much possible to build your self-esteem and change your opinion about yourself with a few steps.

1. Celebrate your small wins

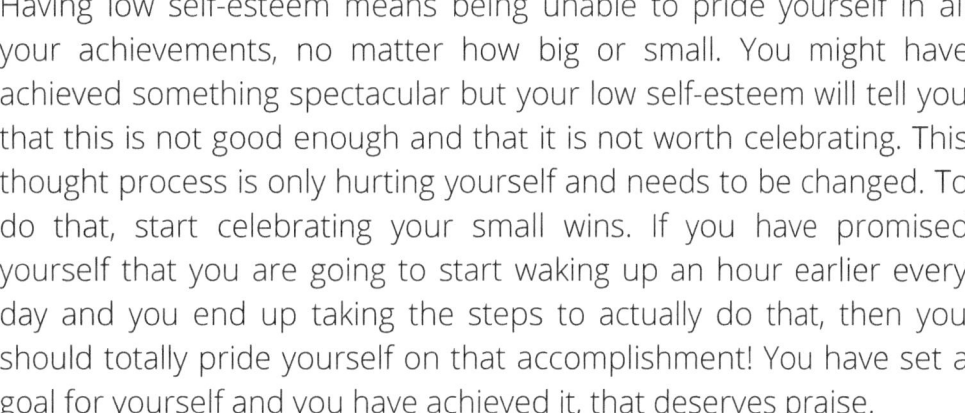

Having low self-esteem means being unable to pride yourself in all your achievements, no matter how big or small. You might have achieved something spectacular but your low self-esteem will tell you that this is not good enough and that it is not worth celebrating. This thought process is only hurting yourself and needs to be changed. To do that, start celebrating your small wins. If you have promised yourself that you are going to start waking up an hour earlier every day and you end up taking the steps to actually do that, then you should totally pride yourself on that accomplishment! You have set a goal for yourself and you have achieved it, that deserves praise.

To keep track of your accomplishments, start noting down your goals and checking them off when you achieve each one. It is easy to set a goal but sometimes we forget to look back when we achieve them and recognize that we actually achieved it and recognize how far we have come. You experience a thrilling sense of accomplishment when you realize your achievements, which causes you to believe in yourself. Having a track record of accomplished goals is hardcore proof that shows you have the capability to do great things and be proud of yourself. Furthermore, you will see that other people will be proud of you too and that your accomplishments are recognized by other people too!

While we do not need to rely on other people's validation to feel accomplished, it does not hurt to have other people pat us on the back and recognize our wins - it makes us feel good! Be sure to pat yourself on the back every time you achieve a goal that you set and you will see your confidence and self-esteem shoot up in no time.

Think back to the past 3 months. What are some small (or big) wins you can celebrate? List them down here.

_____

_____

_____

_____

_____

Think back to the past 3 months. What are some small (or big) wins you can celebrate? List them down here.

Goal	Deadline	Next steps

Goal	Deadline	Next steps

Be sure to keep looking at this list of goals and put a big, fat checkmark next to each one you manage to accomplish.

② Accept compliments (even from yourself)

People with low self-esteem deem themselves unworthy of receiving compliments, mostly because they do not see themselves as "good enough". Consider this situation: you are invited to go to dinner with your friends and you spend around 45 minutes rummaging through your closet looking for the perfect outfit. You try on at least 7 outfits and even though you have a closet full of amazing clothes, you still cannot find anything decent to wear for this. Nothing you try on makes you feel beautiful and you end up feeling worse about yourself. Since you are already late, you throw on any outfit, put on a bit of makeup and take one last look in the mirror. The person looking back at you in the mirror looks stunning: she is radiant and can turn quite a few heads. However, her mind is not convinced of her beauty and she leaves her apartment feeling unexceptional. You reach the restaurant and already 2 of your friends have complimented your makeup and your outfit, however you feel a little uneasy accepting these compliments and tell them that you feel ugly.

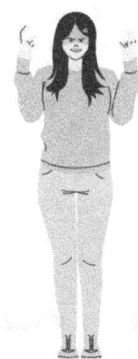

Familiar with this situation? Chances are, most women have felt this way quite a few times in their lives, however women with low self-esteem feel this way quite often. If you have been preyed to feeling this way more than a number of times, then it is likely that your low self-esteem makes you uncomfortable to take the compliment. If you are unable to compliment yourself because you feel ugly, you are likely to be unable to accept compliments from other people, even though they may be genuine compliments.

In order to boost your sense of self-worth, ignore the voice in your head that tells you not to believe people when they complement you. Instead, take the compliment and express your gratitude to the person for recognizing your worth. If someone has taken the time to say something nice to you, they likely mean what they are saying and they would also feel appreciated if you took the compliment and said "thank you so much" with a smile. When you accept the compliment and express your gratitude, it makes it feel more real for your mind as well. By blocking the compliment, you are preventing your mind from seeing how amazing you are, but by letting the compliment in, you are feeding your mind with positivity which will ultimately make you feel great about yourself.

More importantly, if you are ever standing in front of the mirror and your mind is telling you that the reflection staring back at you is unworthy of a compliment, you should shake your head and get rid of those nasty thoughts. Instead, close your eyes, take a deep breath in, exhale, open your eyes and notice all the beautiful aspects about yourself. If you notice some flaws, that is fine! Every human has flaws but that does not mean that you are not beautiful: our imperfections make us perfect. So learn to accept yourself for how beautiful you are and pass yourself a couple of compliments before leaving the house.

Even if you do not fully believe it, just saying them out loud to yourself in the mirror will increase your self-esteem even a little bit compared to if you tell yourself you are not worthy of a compliment. Since you have the freedom to tell yourself anything, why not tell yourself something to make yourself feel good?

By the way, this is applicable to any aspect of yourself, not just the physical beauty part. If someone compliments your personality, something you have accomplished, your relationships, your home or anything that you have put effort into, accept the compliment and bask in the amazing feeling of being seen and appreciated. In due time, you will start to see what a winner you are.

Think of a time when someone complimented you but you were not able to accept it. What happened?

_____

_____

_____

_____

_____

Write down some compliments you can say to yourself now. Write down at least 5.

_____
_____
_____
_____
_____
_____
_____

③ Accept that no one is perfect

Many times, women feel the need to put a lot of pressure on themselves to be perfect - the perfect mother, the perfect girlfriend or wife, the perfect employee or manager, or whatever role they are playing in their lives. Being the "perfect woman" causes so much stress and self-doubt, that there is no room for positive thinking. A woman can feel so bogged down by all the expectations placed on them by other people, as well as themselves, that there is no room left for positive thinking. You feel pressured to meet all of these expectations; and if you fall slightly short, you feel like a failure. You feel as though you could not be that perfect woman who can handle it all without any mistakes.

This cannot be said enough: you need to remember that nobody in this world is perfect. The human experience mandates that we make mistakes and have flaws because that is the only way we can learn and grow into self-actualized people.

Imagine that you looked perfect, you had zero flaws, you had never made any mistakes in your life, you had the perfect lifestyle, you had the perfect set of friends, you were able to do anything and everything, you had the perfect job, you had the perfect house, you had the perfect family, and everything has always been easy for you. Literally everything in your life was perfect.

As ideal as this may sound on paper, think about it for a second. Now answer, how bored would you be with your life? There would be nothing to aim for, nothing to fix, nothing to learn, nothing to work towards. Everything would just be there and you would just be existing the way you are for the rest of your life. That is not what life is about. Life is about constantly reflecting and learning so that you can identify areas within yourself that you can improve and build to live a happy life. Life will not always be easy, the only thing that is constant is change, and so you need to adapt to the events that life will throw at you and just go with it. You do not need to be so hard on yourself because everybody in this world is going through their own journey of self-discovery and growth. Be kind to yourself and lower the unrealistic expectations you have set for yourself.

No matter how much pressure is put on you from external sources, you have the power to decide how much pressure you want to take on. Be compassionate with yourself and relieve some of the pressure. Show up doing your best, and the rest will work itself out however it needs to.

You cannot have control over every outcome; all you can do is deal with whatever you can control in the situation and leave the rest up to the universe to decide. You need to accept that nobody in this world is perfect - everyone has flaws, everybody makes mistakes and life still goes on.

Being imperfect is human. Being human means accepting yourself for your imperfections and still being kind and loving towards yourself regardless. With low self-esteem, you probably give yourself a hard time every time you do not live up to the "perfect woman" image that you have painted in your head; however, that is grounds for negativity and will shatter your confidence even further. You need to realize that if you have not met your expectation one time, that does not mean that you will always not meet it.

You could in fact exceed your expectation another time - you just need to have that confidence in yourself that you are determined to do better for yourself.

If you are not meeting your expectations even a few times, that is completely okay. It just means that you need to alter your expectations of yourself and do your best within your capacity. It is not the end of the world; instead accept that everybody is trying their best and if you alter your expectations to be more manageable for yourself, you will not be falling behind. In fact, being more realistic and compassionate with yourself will help you thrive in a stressful world, because you will be prioritizing your mental wellbeing and encouraging yourself in a positive manner.

Being in a good mental space, instead of a stressful one, will encourage you to do better for yourself because you will be providing yourself with positivity and support. If you ever feel overwhelmed with all the expectations and feel like you are drowning, it can be tough to gather your thoughts. In instances like these, take a deep breath in, exhale and tell yourself that you will be okay, no matter what.

Shatter this image of the "perfect woman" in your head and create an image of a woman who is simply trying her best. If someone is pressuring you to be perfect and it is stressing you out and causing you to doubt your capabilities, you have the right to tell them that their expectations are unrealistic and are causing you to feel overwhelmed.

You are entitled to protect your peace and let other people know that you are doing the best you can. Do this for yourself and you will start to see your self-esteem build up. Trying to be someone you are not will always leave you feeling inadequate. Why make yourself feel this way when you can just show up as your most authentic self and do your best? You will definitely feel better about yourself and you will start to see yourself as a wonderful woman who can conquer the world, even if you are not "perfect".

What expectations do you have of yourself to be perfect?

_____

_____

_____

What expectations do other people have of you to be perfect?

_____

_____

_____

What do you usually tell yourself when you are unable to meet any of these expectations?

_____

_____

_____

Who in your life do you deem to be the "perfect woman"? Why?

_____
_____
_____
_____

Break down the image of the "perfect woman" in your head and create a new image of yourself that includes your strengths and weaknesses. Write down new, more realistic, expectations you can have of yourself that accommodate your weaknesses.

_____
_____
_____
_____

Lastly, write down a positive mantra you can tell yourself when you do not live up to any of these new expectations. Make sure it is forgiving, compassionate, loving and encouraging.

_____
_____
_____
_____

Step out of your comfort zone

Having low self-esteem causes you to take less risk. You are more comfortable with doing the things you have already tried-and-tested so you do not face the wrath of failure. Since your ego is pretty fragile, doing anything unfamiliar might scare you because if it does not go well according to your expectations, then it will just add to your low self-esteem issue. It will be a further justification that you are unable to do things successfully and will lower your confidence further to deter you from having new experiences.

Trying new things broadens your mind to seeing the world in a different light. If you continue to do the same old activities, hang out with the same people, eat the same food, sit in the same chair every day, your life will only be confined to those particular experiences.

Limiting yourself to the monotony of life will not help you think positively, because you will be stuck in the same loop of thoughts with the same events in your life.

The best way to grow as a human being and feed your soul is to expose yourself to something new; sometimes this means doing something with which you are unfamiliar. This might sound scary, but once you conquer the fear of doing something new, you will feel as though you can conquer anything in the world, which will boost your self-esteem.

The best way to grow as a human being and feed your soul is to expose yourself to something new; sometimes this means doing something with which you are unfamiliar. This might sound scary, but once you conquer the fear of doing something new, you will feel as though you can conquer anything in the world, which will boost your self-esteem.

When you accomplish something, a "happy" neurotransmitter called dopamine is released into your bloodstream. Dopamine is in charge of making you feel good when you achieve a goal or successfully take on a challenge because this neurotransmitter has the power to make you feel rewarded. When you step out of your comfort zone to tackle something new, your brain might throw all these thoughts at you that will make you think you will not be able to do it.

You might have a thought about how scary the experience might be or how you might fail at it, or you might have a thought you will regret engaging in this new experience because it might not provide any sort of value to your life. Having all these thoughts and believing them makes the dopamine taste even sweeter when you finally do step out of your comfort zone and live through the experience. You will feel so rewarded; your confidence will shoot up and it will motivate you to gain more experiences.

Imagine you are stuck in a bubble. This bubble always looks the same, feels the same - it even smells the same! You walk around while encased in this bubble and so the world looks the same every single day because you are looking at it through the single perspective of that particular bubble. You will probably start to feel bored or even suffocated staying in this bubble all the time and will crave for something more.

Imagine you are stuck in a bubble. This bubble always looks the same, feels the same - it even smells the same! You walk around while encased in this bubble and so the world looks the same every single day because you are looking at it through the single perspective of that particular bubble. You will probably start to feel bored or even suffocated staying in this bubble all the time and will crave for something more.

Now, imagine popping that bubble and stepping out into the world to look at life from a whole new perspective. You are actually able to do so many more things without that bubble around you and can go and do whatever you like! It will be scary, no doubt, but that breath of fresh air and freedom will also be riveting. Stepping out of your comfort zone will reassure you that the world is your oyster and that you are not trapped by any means.

This will give you self-confidence and motivation to truly start living your life to do the things you have always wanted to do. This self-confidence will make you believe in yourself and also make you realize that you are a person of substance who goes after what they want.

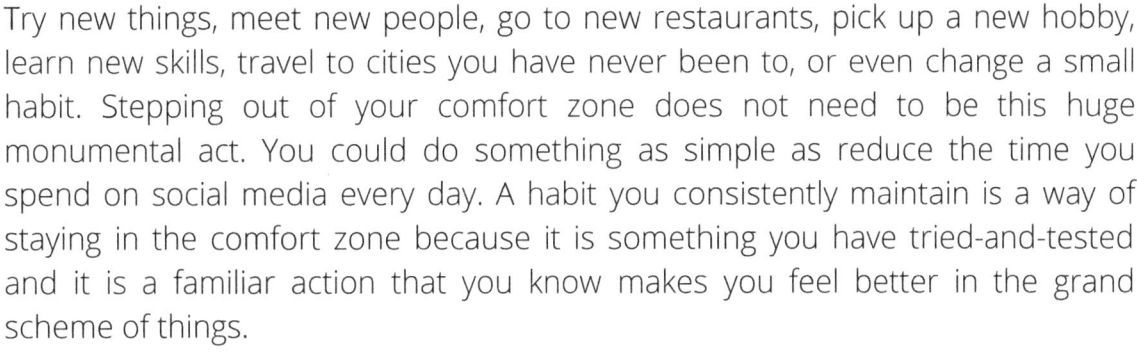

Try new things, meet new people, go to new restaurants, pick up a new hobby, learn new skills, travel to cities you have never been to, or even change a small habit. Stepping out of your comfort zone does not need to be this huge monumental act. You could do something as simple as reduce the time you spend on social media every day. A habit you consistently maintain is a way of staying in the comfort zone because it is something you have tried-and-tested and it is a familiar action that you know makes you feel better in the grand scheme of things.

Due to this, it is normal to be reluctant to change that habit; however, sometimes some habits need to be changed and working to change these habits will fuel your motivation to do something for yourself by stepping out of the comfort zone. Doing something different and effortlessly trying to change something so ingrained takes work and can feel extremely uncomfortable; however, conquering this and changing a habit can make you feel equally as accomplished too.

Step out of your comfort zone and open your mind to something new and uncomfortable; you will see your confidence rise when you are able to do this and your mind will start reframing its thoughts from "I cannot do this" to "this is awesome - I can totally do more of this".

Think about your day-to-day life. What are some habits or routines that you do regularly that you think might not be adding much value to you or might even be harming you?

_____

_____

_____

_____

_____

Write down some things you have always wanted to try or do but have been too afraid to pursue:

_____

_____

_____

_____

_____

_____

Now that you have listed down some of the things you would like to try out, you have a guide for stepping out of your comfort zone. The next step is to plan out when you might try each of these things. Write down when and how you will try each new experience you have listed above:

_____

_____

_____

_____

_____

_____

Set and enforce your boundaries

A lot of the time, people with low self-esteem are unable to think positively because they allow people to cross their boundaries. When you have low self-esteem, you tend to take all the validation you can get from other people because that is your source of truth.

You are unable to see how worthy you are by yourself, so you rely on other people's opinions of you to define that worthiness for you. As a result, you give people what they want so that they will approve of you, even if it means that your own boundaries are crossed.

Being liked and accepted is more important to someone with low self-esteem than standing their ground and putting themselves first. Pleasing someone else will give you the temporary satisfaction of being liked; however, doing this unconsciously reinforces the notion that your needs do not matter, someone else's needs are more important and that love and attention needs to be earned.

Having low self-esteem makes you neglect yourself; this often involves allowing people to do or say things that you are not comfortable with, especially at the expense of your own mental wellbeing. For example, if one of your friends is constantly gossiping and speaking ill about one of your other good friends to you, you would probably feel pretty uncomfortable being in a situation like that.

Your friend may justify this by saying that "she needs to vent" or that this is just "innocent talk"; however, if you feel uncomfortable talking about another friend behind her back, then that means a boundary is being crossed. You might be the type of person that would rather not speak this way about anybody, especially about your friends, and remove yourself from a situation like this.

Low self-esteem means you need to be liked and accepted, and you might fear that telling your friend that you do not want to talk to her about this anymore could result in that friend disapproving and possibly speaking ill of you to someone else or even cutting you out (which is most likely not going to be the case).

Your low self-esteem makes you fear being abandoned, and so you go along and listen to what your friend has to say about your other friend, while neglecting your need to get out of the situation and the discomfort you are experiencing. Neglecting this boundary of yours pushes your self-esteem lower because your mind is telling yourself that your needs are not valued.

In order to boost your self-esteem, you would ideally tell your friend that you are not comfortable having these conversations because you do not like to speak badly about any of your friends. Here, you would be putting your foot down and setting your boundary in order to protect your peace.

If your friend understands this, they will respect your boundary and not involve you in conversations about your other friend. If your friend does not understand why you are setting this boundary, they might say things that could insinuate that your boundary is not important to them and sadly, you will come across people in your life that will not be understanding of your boundaries.

In moments like these, you need to stand your ground and enforce your boundaries. Setting boundaries can even include saying no to events when you are exhausted or not answering calls after getting into bed. No matter what the boundary is, low self-esteem can make you waver to avoid conflict or abandonment, but building your sense of self-worth means being strong and making it known that you will not allow yourself to be put in situations with which you are uncomfortable.

You are entitled to express yourself if something does not sit right with you, and you are totally allowed to remove yourself from a situation that makes you uncomfortable without needing to explain yourself. Your needs are important and people need to know that you will not let them walk all over you. When you set a boundary and stick to it, and you see other people respect that boundary, you start to feel pretty good about yourself. You are finally putting yourself first and your needs are being met. This helps to reinforce your self-esteem because your mind is telling itself that your needs are its number one priority, and it will not allow anything or anyone to harm its peace and sanity. You start to respect yourself more and that increases your sense of self-worth.

Think about some situations that have made you feel uncomfortable:

___

___

___

___

___

What would you have wanted to happen in those situations instead?

___

___

___

___

___

What do you think your boundaries are?

___

___

___

___

___

Can you think of a time when someone crossed a boundary and you let it slide? What happened? ✎

_____
_____
_____
_____

Can you think of a time when someone crossed a boundary and you stood up to them? What happened? ✎

_____
_____
_____
_____

How did you feel when you stood up to this person for ignoring your boundary? ✎

_____
_____
_____

Pick two of the boundaries you have listed above. Based on those boundaries, imagine you are in two difficult situations in which these boundaries are being neglected. What would you tell yourself and the other person that is crossing the line? How would you enforce your boundaries in these situations?

Situation 1:

_____
_____
_____
_____
_____
_____

Situation 2:

_____
_____
_____
_____
_____
_____

Write down a positive mantra that you can tell yourself to self-soothe before you need to enforce a boundary with someone else. Tip: make sure it soothes you but also empowers you to be a strong woman who does not need to be afraid of anybody's negative responses:

_____
_____
_____
_____

6. Engage in some form of physical exercise

Believe it or not, physical exercise can greatly benefit not only your physical health, but also your mental health. Moving your body can pull you into a mental space where you feel good about yourself because you know that you are helping your body and mind be healthy. Taking control over your physical health can positively impact your mental health because your body releases endorphins.

You might have heard this before, but endorphins are chemicals that are released into your bloodstream when you engage in physical exercise. Your brain signals to the body to release this hormone and you start to feel great because this hormone is designed to uplift your mood. You could be having a horrible day, but even a 30-minute workout can turn that frown upside down because of endorphins and self-motivation. Our good old friend dopamine also plays a role because when you work out, you feel like you are achieving something and the reward-based chemical is released, which makes you feel accomplished. Working out helps you clear your mind and prepare you for the rest of the day on a more motivational note.

Apart from endorphins and dopamine, physical exercise helps women cope with body-image issues. The world is moving slowly towards an era of acceptance of any body shape and size, which is a huge step in the right direction. There is more love and encouragement given to all body types and less people are enforcing the model body type on every single woman in the world.

Not every woman has the same body, because every woman's genetic makeup and lifestyle is different. It is impossible to expect every woman in the world to look a certain way in order to live up to society's standard of "beauty", which is why broadening the definition of beauty is so necessary.

While the world is moving in the direction of breaking these standards and recognizing all types of beauty, there are still some people and even brands that believe that women need to look a certain way to be beautiful.

Whether it is shown in the media or spoken about in social settings, if a woman does not meet that specific criteria of beauty, they automatically feel as though they are not beautiful. If you have ever felt like you are not beautiful because of whatever reason, let me first start by telling you that THIS IS ABSOLUTELY NOT TRUE. Every woman is beautiful in her own way, and so are you.

Dealing with body perception issues can take a huge toll on self-esteem. It is a natural human tendency to want to know that you are attractive, because looking good makes you feel good internally about yourself as well. This is not to say that your entire existence is tied to the way you look; however, your perception of your physical appearance does play a role in your level of confidence.

Please note the important term "perception" here. You could be the most attractive woman in the world and every single person out there could want to either be you or be with you, but if you do not see how beautiful you are then you will still have body image issues.

Other people's perceptions of your physical appearance does not matter as much as your own perception of your physical appearance. Almost every woman has gone down that spiral thinking that they are not attractive enough and it can really hamper your self-esteem. If you have been victim to this, take comfort in the fact that you are not alone.

Physical exercise does not always completely fix the body perception issues; however, it does help to build self-confidence when it comes to physical appearance. When you exercise, your mind knows that this will reap benefits for your body. You might be working out in order to get fit or to simply get your body moving and distract yourself from the stress of daily life.

Whatever the reason, your mind knows that one of the by-products of working out will be making you fitter and healthier, which could ultimately lead to your body looking different in a way that you might appreciate.

Engaging in physical exercise reassures your mind that you are taking the necessary steps to take care of your body, which could result in your body and face looking healthier. You gain confidence that because of your actions in your physical workout, you are somehow helping yourself look physically more attractive. Most of the time, working out does make you feel more attractive and so your self-esteem increases and you feel more confident about yourself. You indirectly deem yourself worthy of being happy because you believe that when you look good, you feel good and that great things can happen to you.

It is important to remember, though, that no matter what your body or face looks like, you are still beautiful and you deserve to be happy. Physical exercise is just another means to gaining more confidence about yourself and building your self-esteem.

Have you ever struggled with or currently struggle with body perception issues? If so, what kinds of thoughts do you often have?

_____
_____
_____
_____

How do you feel when you have these thoughts?

_____
_____
_____
_____

Recount a time when you were deeply affected about the way you look and write down how you coped with it at the time:

_____
_____
_____
_____
_____

Do you do any sort of physical exercise now? Write down what you do and how frequently you do it:

_____
_____
_____
_____
_____

If you do exercise, how do you usually feel about yourself afterward?

_____

_____

_____

_____

If you do not workout currently, how do you think you can start incorporating some form of exercise into your routine?

_____

_____

_____

_____

Increasing self-esteem is a surefire way to start thinking positively. When you feel good, you think good, and vice versa. Think about how you view yourself and identify what your inner dialogue sounds like. Reflect on why you feel this way about yourself and work towards being more compassionate, accepting, and loving of yourself. The only person who can give you an authentic ego boost is yourself, and luckily there are ways to do that for the long-run. When your opinion about yourself changes for the better, your thoughts will change for the better, and you will start to act in ways that make your life better too. Keep reminding yourself of what a brilliant and amazing woman you are! You got this.

CHAPTER 5:

SURROUND YOURSELF WITH OTHER ENCOURAGING WOMEN

As clichéd as this may sound, the people around you can truly influence you in a lot of ways. Humans are social beings, and it is natural for us to adapt to the people we frequently interact with and adopt some of their ways of thinking and behaviors, as well as look to them for support to survive this complicated world. We also tend to soak in the energies of other people around us, and this can deeply influence our own energy. Our thoughts and moods can be influenced by others and if we are surrounded by negative people, we absorb that negative energy and start to think negatively too.

One of the reasons we are sometimes so impressionable, even as adults, is we want to feel like we belong. As humans, we crave to be part of a group to have a support system. When we spend enough time with the people in our social networks, we tend to get accustomed to them and adopt some of their personality (even if it is just a tiny part of it) because we unconsciously believe that if we act similarly enough to someone, they will accept us.

Sometimes, this theory does prove to be true; people are more inclined to build friendships and relationships with people similar to them than with those with whom they may not have much in common. Sometimes, people stick to who they are and do not waver from their ideologies and behaviors, however that does not mean that they do not need a support system. They still do. You can be similar or different to people. You still need a strong and suitable support system to get you through your tough days and to lift you up.

The most important aspect of having a support system are the people in it. You could have a large number of friends; however, if they are harming your mental health more than helping it, you should know that these are not the people you want to keep in your inner circle. Imagine this scenario: you are a mother to two children and super swamped with a corporate job. You spend most of your days taking care of the kids and trying to complete all your deliverables at work at a decent hour; however, you somehow do not seem to get the time to do things for yourself or even just relax.

The most important aspect of having a support system are the people in it. You could have a large number of friends; however, if they are harming your mental health more than helping it, you should know that these are not the people you want to keep in your inner circle. Imagine this scenario: you are a mother to two children and super swamped with a corporate job. You spend most of your days taking care of the kids and trying to complete all your deliverables at work at a decent hour; however, you somehow do not seem to get the time to do things for yourself or even just relax.

Most days feel monotonous and can feel as though you are in a rut. However, you are extremely fond of cooking. With the lifestyle you now have, you know you can either run yourself into the ground trying to excel at a job you do not even like, while struggling to give your kids the time and attention they need from a positive mother, or you could pursue something you are passionate about and feel so happy on most days such that this positive energy naturally resonates with the rest of your family as you take care of them. You decide to go with the latter and quit your job to start your very own catering company. It is a huge risk; but you are willing to take that risk in order to give yourself and your children what you all deserve.

Now, imagine telling your inner circle that you are taking this huge step, and they start listing out all the reasons why this is a bad idea. Your friends start to pick at each positive aspect you bring up and crush your dream to make you feel as though you do not have what it takes to succeed. What was once a dream has now gone back to being a scary possibility that your mind does not explore again. In a situation like this, do you think this inner circle can help you think positively? Not really. In fact, these people would only feed your self-doubt and fear, which would make you go down a spiral of negative thoughts every time you choose to take any sort of risk.

Being a part of an encouraging inner circle means telling them your dreams and having those people support you lovingly since this is what will make you happy. Women have been fighting for generations to grab their chance to pursue their passions and climb the success ladder to the top.

Their fellow women should cheer their friends on, not push them off the ladder. In this situation, if you had supportive friends cheering you on and being there to support you along the way, you would feel much more confident about starting a new venture. The devil that is self-doubt will not make as many appearances in your life.

In order to think and feel positively, you need supportive and encouraging women in your close network and here is why:

Women can empathize with what you are struggling with

Many women face similar issues in their daily lives - whether it be regarding inequality in the workplace, feeling overwhelmed and nervous while raising children, heartbreak, or anything else. Women are able to understand what other women are going through. Women are well-equipped with the empathy skill because society deems it "more acceptable" for a woman to process her emotions and talk about her feelings whereas that is sadly not the case for men.

For generations, men have been expected to suppress their emotions and "be strong". Being vulnerable as a man is seen as a weakness in society. Of course, things are slowly but surely changing, and people today are realizing that men showing their vulnerabilities to the world should be normalized, just as it is for women; however, due to the long history of gender biases, it is the women who have been taught that it is okay to show their emotions more than men.

Research suggests that women may be able to empathize and process their emotions more effectively than men because of the way their brains process information. Most women tend to focus on their feelings when they are in a negative situation, whereas most men tend to look at their feelings from a more logical point of view and attempt to analyze the problem and immediately start looking for solutions.

This is not to say that all women think this way and all men think in this way; however, research has suggested that it is common for most women and men to think in this respective manners and process their emotions slightly differently from each other.

Since most women are a little more in-tune with their feelings and are better able to express themselves, having encouraging women in your inner circle gives you a good soundboard for you to vent. Sometimes, life can get really tough, and even though you might have the strength to deal with it all by yourself, it is usually beneficial to share your experiences with your close network because even though they may not be able to fix the problem for you, they will at least motivate and encourage you, as well as give you compassion. Talking to someone who can relate to you better gives you reassurance to know that you are not alone. Other women have faced similar issues to you and simply talking about it can help you feel so much lighter, almost as if a dark cloud has been lifted from your chest. Confiding in a fellow woman can bring you added confidence and support you might not be able to get from anywhere else, because women stick together and support each other.

Recount a time when you were confiding in a female friend and she empathized with you:

_____

_____

_____

_____

_____

_____

You feel a sense of belonging

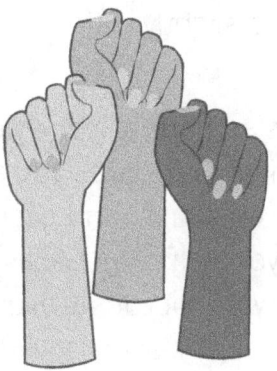

Since most women can relate to each other about certain things, you feel as though you are part of a group. You have a sense of belonging when these women you interact with are your people. Sometimes, only women can relate to other women about certain topics, and when you find your band of supportive women, you feel empowered as a woman. It is human nature to want to belong to a certain group because it ensures our survival.

We learn about things we may never have dealt with before; we gain new experiences as we meet more people, and we feel safe knowing that there are people out there who have our backs. Feeling like we belong increases our mental wellbeing because we avoid the brunt of isolation. Everybody needs at least one person in their life to interact with; otherwise life can get pretty lonely. Having your fellow women by your side makes you feel part of a group, which gives you more confidence to conduct your life in a fulfilling manner.

Imagine that you do not have any encouraging women in your close inner circle. You would go through life fine, but you would miss the sense of connection to someone who can relate to you on a level that your husband, father, brother or male friend might not be able to. Feeling as though you do not belong can make you feel frustrated because you would feel like nobody gets you. Not belonging actually has negative side effects to your mental wellbeing: it can cause you to get into conflicts with your significant other, children, parents or even coworkers. It can demotivate you and harm your performance at work or at school. It can also affect the attention and support you give to your children. It can lead to symptoms of depression or anxiety, as your thoughts tend to turn negative, fearful, and/or hopeless due to loneliness.

Being a part of an empowering group of women gives you the confidence to know that you can conquer the world just like other amazing women. As you interact with these special women, you start to believe in yourself and think, if other women can attain happiness and success in their lives, why couldn't I?

Feeling like you belong to an amazing group of women inspires you to go after the things you want and deserve, and you will have your friends by your side to cheer you on because they can understand where you are coming from.

Having a close-knit group of women support you during the different stages in your life makes you believe that you are not alone, but you are supported, which can uplift your mood and reframe your thoughts to become more positive. You believe that there is space for you in the world and that you have a purpose that positively impacts the people who are close to you. You belong and you matter.

Do you have a group of women that you interact with regularly with whom you feel you belong? Who are they and what are they like?

_____

_____

_____

How do you feel when you spend time with these women?

_____

_____

_____

Women can be experts at uplifting other women

In a world so distracted and fast-paced as ours, we sometimes get lost in the crowd and bogged down by the challenges of everyday life. You could be battling so many wars in your life that the entire world looks like a battlefield you need to tread through without taking time to protect and take care of yourself first. The wounds you bear from these battles end up picking you apart piece by piece, and it can be excruciatingly painful to see the light at the end of the tunnel.

When life has you down, you start to think that nothing will get better for you and your life is destined to always have challenges. Your mind starts throwing these daunting intrusive thoughts your way, and ultimately you are too wounded to fight those too. You start to feel defeated and surrender to your negative thoughts and stressful situations. This even causes you to doubt and neglect yourself and ultimately lose any hope of being that confident woman you want to be.

For situations like these, spending time with supportive women can go a long way because they can uplift you like no other. When a woman is in need, it is implied that others will stick together and pull their fellow woman out of her funk. Empathy, compassion, care, and ambition are all traits that women embody, which they use to motivate other women when they are feeling down about their lives.

You are a goddess, and only another goddess can look into your eyes and feel your pain to the extent that they feel as though they are experiencing what you are going through as well. They are emotionally perceptive, and they know exactly what you need to hear and what you need to do to start feeling better about yourself and your life again.

Hearing a simple "girl, you got this" from another woman can make you feel so much better. A woman usually knows how to appreciate the good things in life, and so they are easily able to highlight all your amazing qualities that make you, you!

Even if your group of women do not have a way with words, they could be great at taking you out and making you have a good time. Simply just sitting with you and keeping you company with a tub of ice cream when you most need it can give you a sense of comfort that will lift your spirits.

Having your girls by your side means having supportive women who want to see you happy and succeed. If you have women in your life who are waiting for you to mess up so that they can make you feel bad about yourself, you already know that these women are not meant for you and you need to cut them out.

There is no need for toxicity; and if you find the right women, you can lead a very happy life knowing that the people in it are looking out for you, just as you would for them. Whether they uplift your mood by telling you how amazing you are or by distracting you from your pain for a little while, supportive women are ultimately giving you the strength and confidence to know that you will be okay and you can be happy. You just need to believe in yourself and have a little faith.

Recount a time when a female friend of yours was feeling down. What did you say to her to uplift her spirits?

_____

_____

_____

_____

If you were feeling horrible, what would you want your female friend(s) to do to make you feel empowered?

_____

_____

_____

Other women can provide you with a fresh perspective

When you are struggling with toxicity in your mind and life, it can be hard to untangle yourself from that sticky web of negative thoughts. It can feel like the more you try to fight those thoughts, the more the web pulls you in to the point where it feels almost impossible to escape. Going down that negative thought spiral can lead you to some dark places, and it can be quite strenuous to get out of those places by yourself. Even if you are not in a particularly tough spot, feeling that you are in a rut and life does not spark your fire anymore can leave you feeling hopeless and languished.

Since you are the most involved in your life, you look at your life from a single perspective and develop thoughts, emotions, and behaviors based on that specific point of view. Looking at life from a single perspective is like wearing tinted glasses and seeing the world in just one color. You live your life thinking that the world can only exist in this color because you have become so accustomed to that one color that any other color seems out of reach.

Encouraging and supportive women can provide you with fresh perspectives that you may not have explored before. If a fellow woman has gone through something similar, she might be able to give you some insight into how she coped with that situation, which should help you see that there are tried-and-tested alternative solutions available that could work for you too. If a woman has not gone through something similar, it might be slightly difficult for her to completely understand what you are going through; however, she can provide you with a fresh way of looking at the situation that you may not have considered. As you are so deeply involved in the situation, it is hard to consider another perspective because your tinted glasses are only showing one color; however, a supportive friend can provide you with another pair of glasses that highlights more than just the one color, and suddenly life seems to be filled with possibilities.

Sometimes, you need that little push from women who care about you to realize that things can get better; you just need to look at life in another way. Ultimately, perception is reality so you can either choose to perceive life in a manner that makes you think negatively, or you can choose to perceive life to be a beautiful journey, in which ups and downs both happen.

Whatever you are going through, it is important to look at multiple perspectives so you can see life from a more holistic view. If you want to start thinking more positively, adopting a more optimistic perspective rather than a negative one would be best, and fellow encouraging women are perfect for bringing these positive perspectives to light if you are struggling.

Think about a situation in your life right now that is not the easiest to deal with. What is your perspective on it as of today?

_____
_____
_____
_____
_____

Does your perspective learn more towards the negative or the positive?

_____
_____
_____
_____
_____

Recount a time when a fellow woman you knew was going through something and you provided a more positive perspective for her to consider. What did you tell her? How do you think it made her feel?

_____

_____

_____

_____

_____

Think of a time when you were viewing the world through tinted glasses - did a friend of yours provide a fresh perspective? How did it feel?

_____

_____

_____

_____

_____

Can help with better decision-making

Everyone's life is their own. We are the puppet masters of our own lives and so we are the ones who get to decide how we react to all the situations that life decides to throw at us. Sometimes, because we are human beings and not robots, we might make some impulsive decisions based on intense emotional reactivity to a stressful situation, which could end up hurting us instead of helping.

At times like this, when there is no one to turn to at that moment, your brain works at 200 miles per hour, and you end up making a decision that you thought would be good in the heat of the moment. However, most of the time, you face the consequences later, and they are usually not good.

Having empowering women in your life can be beneficial because they can lend a helping hand in your decision-making process. Let us look at an example of how women can help with this. Imagine that you were in a pretty serious relationship with a guy for about three years, and you both recently broke up. The break-up was mutual and you have been taking your time to process the loss of the relationship and working your way through the self-healing journey. One day, you open up social media and you see a photo of your ex with a new woman. They do not exactly look platonic; it looks like they are probably dating. Understandably, this hurts you and you start to fill up with anxiety, sadness, rage and a sense of betrayal too. Your heightened emotions make you want to say all of these nasty things to him so you start to type out an unpleasant text message.

Stop here for a second. If you were to send that nasty message to him, he would know that the break-up still affects you and that he has power over your emotions. It would also make him feel as though he is not allowed to move on with his life when in actuality he is allowed to and probably thinks this is the best way for him to move forward, and so he would start to face the wrath of your message and feel horrible about doing what he needs to do to move forward with his life.

Lastly, it also does not reflect well on you to send him that nasty message because the more emotionally mature thing to do would be to deal with your reactions and not project them onto him.

If you saw this photo on social media and instead reached out to a friend first and told them how you felt and what you were intending to do, she could steer you in a better direction because she can be objective about the situation. She can reason with you and help you realize that maybe sending that message is a bad idea.

She will tell you all the reasons why you should not do this and while she is telling you all of this, your mind has a few minutes to cool off and look at the situation more rationally. Waiting just a few more minutes can change your decision-making process and can prevent you from making a mistake that you would regret.

Your female friends most likely understand your impulsivity, because chances are they have also been tempted to act impulsively a couple of times in their own lives due to heightened emotions too. This is why they are the best people to help you take a step back and rethink your impulsive decisions because they might have experienced the consequences themselves or can foresee what might happen if you made a drastic decision and acted upon it without thinking it through.

Your fellow goddesses help you slow down for a second and rationalize whether you are happy making this decision, and that is a beautiful bond to have with the women around you. They support you and they care for you, so they look out for you to ensure you do not end up causing more pain in your life than is already present.

Reflect on a time when you wanted to act impulsively but a friend of yours stopped you from making a bad decision:

___

___

___

___

___

If you had gone ahead with that impulsive decision, how would you have felt about it afterwards?

___

___

___

___

___

They can uplift your mood and bring some fun into your life!

Last but not least, having uplifting women around you is, plain and simple, awesome! Having a few female friends that you trust, enjoy spending time with and can confide in makes your life feel so much more enriching. Even if you are feeling down in the dumps and do not want to talk about what is bothering you, your circle of encouraging women can literally just be there to distract you and take you out for a night on the town. Women are blessed with a multitude of skills - from being able to talk about emotions to living life in the moment and being there for their girlfriends.

One of the best nights of your life could be with your group of girls. Having those bonds with women who uplift your mood can help decrease feelings of loneliness, fear and insecurity. By sharing memorable experiences with your friends, you are enriching your life with positivity. Laughing, telling jokes, sharing secrets, asking for advice, even playing games are all part of having fun with your girlfriends and you feel closer to them. Having deep connections like these make you believe that life can be great if you spend time with authentic and genuine women.

In order to truly have fun with your friends, you need to feel comfortable around them and be able to be your true self. This means keeping women in your network who want the best for you. There are many people, including women, who are not well-versed with the art of self-reflection and so they project their unhappiness onto other people in order to feel better about themselves. You will cross paths with women like these, but it is up to you to recognize them and decide whether you want them in your inner circle. If they provide a certain purpose for you that helps you think positively, then that's great!

However, more often than not, you will find that people like these can do more harm for your mental health than good. Embarking on the journey of positive thinking means cutting out people who may be toxic for you and welcoming a more supportive group of women. It will be difficult to remove some people from your life; however, it is better for your wellbeing in the long-term. You do not need anybody dragging you down, constantly having to fight for yourself and make a conscious effort each time to think positively (even though someone is giving you a reason not to) can be extremely emotionally exhausting!

If you find yourself often feeling worse after meeting someone than how you felt before you met them, that is your cue to reduce the number of interactions you have with this person; otherwise you will be spending most of your mental energy trying to justify why your friendship with her is beneficial for you when you know deep down that it is not. Lying to yourself about certain people to keep the peace is more draining than simply doing what is best for you and cutting them out. Removing toxicity makes room for positive women to enter and change your life.

Think about the women in your life who are most important to you. What are they like? How do you usually feel after you meet each one of them? Write down your experiences below:

_____

_____

_____

_____

Are there any women in your life that prevent you from thinking positively? What do they usually say or do?

_____

_____

_____

_____

If there are some toxic women in your life who make you feel worse than you would like to feel, then think about how you would like to maintain those friendships moving forward. No one is worth compromising your mental wellbeing and confidence.

CHAPTER 6:

CHALLENGE YOUR NEGATIVE THOUGHTS WITH POSITIVE ONES

This might be one of the hardest yet most rewarding steps to take in order to start thinking positively. Positive thinking comes when you are able to identify your negative thoughts, challenge them, and then ultimately reframe them to be more in-tune with reality. Our thoughts have a way of distorting reality so they can present us with negativity. It is easy for us to go down the rabbit hole of negative thinking with just one thought because our minds are experts at making that one thought convincing enough to make us look at our realities through a false lens.

These negative thoughts string themselves together to formulate a false narrative that further pushes you into an abyss of negativity, one that might be vastly different from what your reality actually looks like. As mentioned, perception is reality, and if you are allowing your negative thoughts to rule over you, then your reality will look pretty bleak. However, if you decide to take charge over deciding which thoughts hold power over you, then you will be able to change your outlook on life to a more positive one.

The first step is to identify which thoughts are not serving you well. Thousands of thoughts enter our minds every single day, and a lot of them serve the purpose of making you think the worst. Sticking to these thoughts can make us lead a miserable life because we are literally choosing to believe the thoughts that our mind is conjuring up. Instead, we need to identify when a negative thought has appeared that is not helpful. In order to do that, you need to look at the thought more objectively - prevent yourself from falling into the trap of allowing the thought to overwhelm you, and instead ask yourself if this thought is helpful. For example, a thought such as, "I am never going to make enough money", enters your mind, and it starts to really upset you. Before you believe that thought to be the truth, ask yourself, "is this thought helping me?"

When you ask yourself this question about negative thoughts, most of the time the answer will be no. A thought telling you that you will never in your entire lifetime make enough money is unhelpful because it limits you to believe that the current situation will always be your reality. It is insinuating that your life will never change, and all of us know that the only thing that is constant in life is change.

This thought is unhelpful because it sets you up for failure right from the start, stopping you from taking any steps you would have otherwise wanted to change your life. For a thought like this, you need to recognize that it is an unhelpful negative thought only serving to drag you down, and you need to simply just label it as "unhelpful".

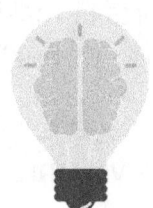

Once you have labeled your thought to be unhelpful, you can take it one step further and label the category of the thought. Since this thought has to do with the inability to increase your income, you could label the thought as "unhelpful cannot-make-money thought" and park it.

Labeling the thought and categorizing it creates distance between you and the thought, which provides you with time and space to decide whether this thought really needs to hold that much value in your mind.

When you have labeled the thought, you will now be able to see just how unlikely it is to have this thought to be true. You do not become your thoughts, you instead start to see them for what they are from a distance - just thoughts. Not the truth, not predictions, just thoughts that come and go. Instead of getting lost in the thought, try exploring where a thought might be coming from and look at it from a perspective of curiosity.

What triggered this thought? Starting from the beginning of what was happening around you when the thought came up might help you decipher why you are thinking this way. Once you identify what might have triggered your thought, dig deeper into why. Think back to your past and all the other times you have had this thought and ask, when do these thoughts usually come about? You can go back further and reflect on experiences in your life that might have caused some pain or insecurity that could have given birth to this thought.

For example, if you often get the thought that you will never be able to have a steady relationship, you should first label this thought as an unhelpful relationship thought. Once you have created a little bit of distance between you and the thought, you can start to explore why you get this thought.

Do you usually get this thought when you see happy couples around you? Do you get this thought every time you open up a dating app? Identify when you usually get this thought and go from there. Introspect on your life and what you have been through. Have you been in a relationship with a man before who has been emotionally inconsistent? Have you seen your parents go through a messy divorce as a young teen? Investigate what life events could have contributed to the formation of this sticky thought. Speaking to a therapist can aid you in this process, however if you are unable to access a therapist at this point in time, this is a self-help process you could try to do for yourself.

Try doing a practice round for one thought now.

Write down a negative or uncomfortable thought you get often:

_____

_____

_____

_____

Label this thought as unhelpful and categorize it:

_____

_____

_____

_____

_____

When do you usually get this thought?

_____

_____

_____

Write down any past life experiences that you think might have contributed to the formation of this thought:

_____

_____

_____

_____

How do you usually feel when this thought comes around?

_____

_____

_____

How do you usually cope with it? ✒

___

___

___

___

Now that you have practiced the art of exploring the root cause of your thought, we can move on to learning how to reframe that thought into a more realistic and positive one. Many times, our negative thoughts are irrational and unrealistic; however, our low self-esteem or sense of hopelessness makes us believe these thoughts to be true, even though they are far from what reality might suggest. The goal here is to get in touch with a more realistic point of view and reconfigure the thought to match that reality. Instead of assuming that the thought is true and that life is all doom and gloom, try shifting your focus to a less uncomfortable point of view.

Taking the unhelpful relationship thought as an example, instead of dwelling on "I will never have a steady relationship", change the words to be less absolute and negative. Never is a strong word and you cannot predict the future, so change the wordings of the thought to be a bit more flexible. Also, change the narrative of the thought to be encouraging more than discouraging, while keeping in mind your reality.

So "I will never be in a steady relationship" changes to "I am not in a steady relationship now, but that could change one day". You are not blatantly lying to yourself by saying this, you are simply stating the facts and encouraging yourself a little bit too.

The reality of the situation is that you are not in a steady relationship right now, but the reality also dictates that this might not be forever. No one knows what the future holds, so instead of predicting negative outcomes, why not predict positive ones? You live in your mind, so why choose to live in a mind with negative thoughts when you can take the steps to change those thoughts into more realistic and hopeful ones? The more you do this, the lighter and more positive your world will begin to feel.

You could even offer yourself an alternate thought, such as "I believe I am going to be in a steady relationship soon". It is not an exact prediction, as you are stating that you believe something will happen, but it is a way of reassuring you that better things are coming. You have some level of hope to live off of during your days that can keep you going.

Try doing this exercise now.

Use that same negative thought that you wrote down earlier and reframe it to a more realistic and encouraging thought below:

_____

_____

_____

_____

_____

_____

_____

_____

Now, repeat this thought to yourself 5 times.

Never underestimate the power a thought has over your mind. If it is positive, then it will most likely leave you feeling more positive than a negative thought would. Think about a thought, change the words and start uplifting your spirits. We only live once, so why should we allow our minds to constantly pull us down, when we can try our best to guide our mind to lift us up?

To keep track of your progress, you keep a thought journal. Writing down these negative thoughts allows you to keep track of the kinds of thoughts you have on a daily basis.

When you see these thoughts written down, they start to lose their power because that negative energy in your mind has now been transferred onto paper (or a digital notepad). Seeing those words in a more physical form makes them seem less threatening because you see your thoughts as words, not threats. Once you have written down your negative thoughts, you look at the words objectively and change them to make them more rational and uplifting.

You could create columns on a page - one side be for the negative thought and the other side be for the reframed positive thought. That way, you can compare the two. You will be able to see just how different your mindset can be just by changing a few words.

Try doing this now with 5 thoughts. Write down 5 negative thoughts, and then write down a reframed realistic and encouraging thought in the next column:

Negative thought	Reframed thought

As you keep writing down your thoughts and reframing them, your mind gets used to this process, and it becomes automatic. The more you practice a cognitive pattern, the more it gets embedded into your brain. Your brain creates new neural pathways to allow you to easily think and behave in ways more automatically. If you are used to reacting angrily to situations and you start meditating and make a conscious effort to react to situations more calmly, your brain will start to create neural pathways based on your calmer behaviors.

As these neural pathways get stronger, they become your automatic behavioral and cognitive pathways in life situations. Instead of going down the angry neural pathway, you go down the calmer neural pathway due to practice and habituation.

The same concept applies to reframing negative thoughts. As you keep doing this, your brain gets habituated to reframing negative thoughts and soon enough your mind does it so easily that you might not even realize how quickly your negative thoughts are being transformed into more positive ones.

Tell yourself positive affirmations

Another wonderful way to change your thought processes is to say positive affirmations to yourself on a regular basis. Positive affirmations are statements that exude uplifting sentiments that make you feel confident, happier and motivated to love and accept yourself for who you are. You can say them about any aspect of yourself or your life - the statements just need to make you feel better. Simple "I am..." statements are easy enough for you to come up with and to repeat to yourself in order to boost your self-esteem and happiness levels.

For example, you could say to yourself "I am kind". That is a positive affirmation because you are affirming the fact that you have a positive quality within you that makes you such a wonderful woman. You are recognizing the positivity within you and harnessing that to provide you with the confidence to know that you truly are amazing.

If you tell yourself positive things about yourself and your life, you will start to believe them. That beats telling yourself discouraging things, because your mind will start to believe those negative statements and make you live your life with low self-esteem, low levels of life satisfaction and unhappiness. Instead, positive affirmations are statements you say to yourself, which ultimately make you navigate your way through life believing that you truly are amazing.

How does this come into practice in reality? Let us pretend that you are telling yourself that you are an extremely smart woman. This is a positive affirmation that solidifies the fact that your intelligence goes beyond just books and that you can figure out this thing called life in a manner that is beneficial for you.

Telling yourself you are smart gives you the confidence to have meaningful and interesting conversations with other people, which not only shows the world how insightful you are, but can also provide you with new knowledge on different topics that you might not have been familiar with just through your intelligent curiosity.

Moreover, believing that you are a smart woman will make you welcome new skills into your life that can make your life more fulfilling. For example, if you are interested in the world of computer science, the confidence you have in your ability to learn will motivate you to take some coding classes and practice. If you were telling yourself that you were not smart and you did not truly believe it, you would most probably shy away from learning a new skill or having conversations with interesting people, which would result in you not diving into things that could potentially make you excited about life.

Repeating negative statements to yourself can demotivate you and cause you to engage in certain behaviors that discourage you from living your best life. Positive affirmations have a strong ripple effect on the actions you take in your daily life and can actually push you towards the ideal life you want to have.

There is no limit to how many positive affirmations you can say to yourself. These can be the same every day, or you can add or remove some as you go along - the world of positivity and encouragement is your oyster!

To start with, write down 7 positive affirmations you can say to yourself everyday:

_____

_____

_____

_____

_____

_____

_____

To keep this interesting, think of some creative ways you can tell yourself these positive affirmations. You could keep one as your wallpaper on your phone one day so that you can look at one for the day and absorb that positivity, then change your wallpaper the next day to reflect a new positive affirmation. It is a simple yet necessary reminder to keep seeing the wonderful qualities within yourself, without having to put in too much effort.

You could come up with a morning ritual wherein you say 3 positive affirmations to yourself in the mirror as you are getting ready in the morning, so that you start your day feeling awesome about yourself. See what works for you and repeat positive affirmations to yourself in ways that you think would resonate with you best.

What are some creative ways you can say positive affirmations to yourself? Think of 3 fun ways:

_____

_____

_____

Next time you find yourself going down the negative thought spiral, take a deep breath and look at each thought objectively. Work through the steps you have learned above and reframe each thought to a more positive and realistic one, and repeat positive affirmations to reassure yourself of how amazing you really are. The most important person you need validation from is you because you are ultimately the one who gives yourself the strength to believe that you are truly extraordinary. Validating yourself will result in a drastic shift in your mindset which will allow you to start thinking positively about pretty much every aspect of your life.

Your thoughts are the mantras you live by, so make sure they are lifting you up and not dragging you down. You have the power to decide what thoughts can control you. Take the reins on your mind and watch your mindset change.

CHAPTER 7:

MASTER THE ART OF MEDITATION

For most of the day, especially for a serial overthinker, the mind is either lost in thought or going on autopilot. You could be entertaining every single thought that pops into your head and going down a trajectory of overthinking that strays you away from the present moment, which results in being unable to pull yourself to focus on the present reality. Or your mind could be so filled with thoughts and your daily routine could be so packed that your mind runs on its own without you consciously having any control because your mind cannot handle everything all at once, so it just runs on its own without you even realizing what you are doing.

Being on autopilot can even be a result of feeling like you are stuck in a monotonous rut that you cannot get out of, and so your mind just does what it does every single day without you having to make an effort to make a decision or take an action consciously. Running on autopilot makes you miss the current moments of your life because you do not absorb what is happening in the present.

Both ways, your mind is somewhere other than the given moment; this is an easy way to lose out on what life has to offer you, which can lead to you feeling unfulfilled with your life. Negative thinking and feelings of hopelessness can arise when you feel unfulfilled, which can make it extremely difficult to see silver linings.

A great way to think more positively is to master the art of meditation. Meditation is the practice of bringing yourself to the present moment and allowing your mind to simply observe and focus your attention on what is currently in existence. Meditating allows you to bring your mind to a calm state and expand your awareness internally as well as externally.

For example, let us say that you are walking through a beautiful garden - there are all sorts of colorful flowers, some that you do not even recognize, and the air smells of freshly-cut grass and the sky is bright blue with the sun smiling down at you. It is a beautiful day; however, your mind does not realize how beautiful this day is. Instead, your mind is too busy rummaging through an old box of painful memories and embarrassing conversations and unrealistic predictions to recognize the beauty of the present moment.

Although you are walking through this breathtaking garden, your mind is solely focused on all the information your brain is spewing up to make you feel uncomfortable. Meditation, however, would hold your brain's hand and guide it back to this beautiful moment.

Meditation is an exercise that you need to keep practicing to be able to observe your current circumstance and take it all in without placing judgment. Oftentimes, the thoughts and emotions that pop up are based on judgments that we place on our current circumstances.

When we judge something, we are either placing an opinion based on past experiences or predicting an outcome, which would skew our perception of reality.

In the example of the garden, you could place judgment on a fountain that you see. Instead of enjoying the intricacies of the fountain, your mind might predict that you will get sprinkled by the fountain, which could worry you as you do not have a spare change of clothes. Instead of living in the moment, you are attached to a judgment of an event that could potentially ruin the moment for you.

Meditation solves that problem - it teaches you to let the present exist as it is by simply observing and not allowing your thoughts to run wild. If they do run wild, then meditation teaches you how to not run away with them and simply let them come and go. You are purely seeing the moment for what it is and hopefully absorbing the positivity that comes from it.

Meditating is not all that hard to master. It takes time and practice to be skillful at it, but it is something very attainable for people who are determined to not let their thoughts and emotions govern their lives. A good first step to practicing meditation is to practice deep breathing. The core of meditation is to focus on something in the present, and focusing on your breath is a surefire way to train your mind to shift its attention to the moment.

Find a comfortable spot and sit in a position that is most relaxing for you. Close your eyes and start taking some deep breaths. Inhale through your nose for about 5 seconds and then exhale through your mouth for around 6 seconds. While you are taking your deep breath in, shift your attention to that inhale.

How does the air smell? What temperature is it? What does your inhale sound like? Observe these little aspects about your inhale without attaching any judgment. Similarly, observe your exhale: how does it feel against your lips when you exhale? Do your muscles relax when you exhale?

Observe and be in the moment. Keep being attentive to your breathing. It is natural for you to encounter thoughts along the way, and that is okay! You are human; your mind cannot switch off and meditation might still be a new practice for you, so be compassionate with yourself. If a thought comes along while you are trying to focus on your breathing, just acknowledge that a thought has popped up and bring your attention back to your breath.

You do not need to get lost in that thought; simply tell yourself "oh look, that thought is here" and walk away from it to get back to focusing on your breathing. Training your mind to focus on your breathing is a great way to bring yourself back to reality and give your mind a little break from all the thought spirals it might be jumping into. Since you breathe at all times during the day, you can literally meditate for a few minutes anytime and anywhere, since you have your breath at your disposal.

Try meditating now for 5 minutes. Take deep breaths in through your nose and exhale from your mouth. Do this for 5 whole minutes and try to bring your awareness back to your breathing every time your mind starts to wander. Do this, and then write down how you feel after meditating:

_____

_____

_____

_____

_____

Mastering the meditation with your breath gives you the foundation to meditate even if you are not solely focusing on your breath and have multiple distractions within and around you. Since your mind is conditioned to know how to focus on one thing, it will be able to focus on even a candle flame or an interesting wallpaper design. Literally anything can be your focal point during meditation and this will further train your mind to be aware of what is in front of you.

Using the candle flame as an example, you can focus on its color, its height, how it flickers and the shadows it produces. Observing these little aspects about the candle flame and labeling these aspects without judgment makes your brain slow down so that it can absorb what is present in front of you at this moment.

Focusing on one thing leaves little space for unnecessary thoughts to barge in; however, it is not impossible, so when these thoughts do come in and try to interrupt you, remember to simply acknowledge that they are entering your mindspace without getting roped into them or fighting to push them away.

Interacting with them on a deeper level in any way will pull your focus away, and that is the opposite intention of meditation. The goal is to simply allow your thoughts to exist without getting so affected by them while focusing on the present moment. Meditation also gives you the concentration skill you need while being productive; you get better at focusing on a task without allowing distractions to pull you away, which makes you more efficient, productive and ultimately feel good about your work ethic.

To help you while meditating, picture your thoughts as raindrops on a window. There will be many raindrops that fall onto the window of your mind; however, instead of focusing on each raindrop that rolls down the window, you can simply observe them and let them roll down as they please without letting them bother you.

Visualizing your thoughts as something that is non-threatening will help you allow them to simply exist, even if they are negative thoughts that could affect you. Think about it - would you hold on to or fight a raindrop? No, you probably would not. Think about what visual you would prefer to have for your thoughts and keep this visual in mind when you meditate the next time unwanted thoughts come by. Visualize them coming and then going without you sticking to them.

What do you think you can visualize your thoughts as?

_____

_____

_____

_____

_____

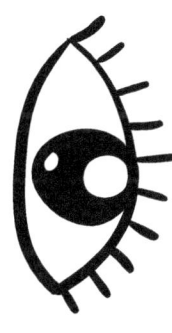

Visualization is a helpful technique to use during meditation. Although it transports you to a different reality within your mind, it still sharpens the skill of focus and attention. The key to visualization during meditation is to picture a place that makes you happy and calm. You could picture yourself at a lake with the sound of the water flowing and crickets with bright blue skies, or you could picture a scenic view of a beach at sunset - whatever visual makes you feel happiest and most relaxed.

While visualizing this scene, focus on your five senses. What do you see? What sounds do you hear? What can your mind smell? What do you taste? What do you feel when you touch something in that visual? You create a surreal experience for yourself through focus, even though it is all in your mind. Your brain is conditioned to know how to center attention on particular details.

What place(s) would you visualize while meditating to feel happy and calm?

_____

_____

Getting in touch with your five senses is a perfect way to stay grounded in reality in real life too. If you are getting lost in your thoughts, you can do a quick grounding exercise by observing your five senses. No matter where you are and what you are doing, if you feel like your mind is dealing with a lot, take a minute to look around you and experience the moment as it is right now using each of your senses.

Doing this exercise will bring your mind back to the basic core of existence and give you space to breathe away from everything that was initially inundating you. In whatever form you choose to meditate, the goal is to bring your awareness back to the present so your mind can settle down and return to a calmer state.

Try doing it now. Observe the area around you right now and list down the following:

5 things you can see:

_____

_____

_____

_____

_____

4 things you can hear:

_____

_____

_____

_____

3 things you can feel/touch:

_____

_____

_____

2 things you can smell:

_____

_____

1 thing you can taste:

_____

When you feel as though you are stuck in the middle of a topsy-turvy whirlwind of emotions and thoughts, just take a step back, close your eyes, and breathe. Focus on your breath and bring your focus back to the present, and let all your thoughts and emotions pass you by.

They might scare you, but work on accepting the fact that not all thoughts and emotions will make you feel good. It is all part of the psychological experience to feel good and bad emotions; however, do not let this make you think that you need to latch on to each and every thought and emotion that comes your way.

Meditation helps you realize that not every single thought that pops up needs your attention. You have the power to simply let the thought exist without giving it your focus. When you do this, you give that negative thought or emotion less power over you, which ultimately trains your mind to be resilient against uncomfortable thoughts and feelings that are designed to tear you down.

You are easily able to think positively because you will have the power to simply let all the negativity around you just exist without letting it get to you, and instead focus on the thoughts and emotions that make you feel good. You are the master of your mind, and meditation is your tool.

Sometimes, it makes it easier to remember to meditate if you fix a specific time of the day to meditate.

When do you think you can allocate time to meditate every day?

_____

_____

_____

How long would you like to meditate for?

_____

_____

_____

CHAPTER 8:

NAVIGATE THROUGH THE WORLD WITH KINDNESS

Being a positive person has many contributing factors; however, one factor that makes being positive easier is kindness. Being kind involves behaviors that show consideration for others; it is a selfless quality that allows a person to show compassion to someone else. A lot of the time, we are so absorbed with our own lives that we forget to check in with other people around us. This does not make us bad people at all! With the way the world moves today in its fast-paced nature, it is normal to get lost in the struggles of daily life that we either forget to check in with others or simply do not have the energy or time to give to someone else. That said, whenever we do interact with others, it is necessary to do so with kindness to maintain a harmonious and positive relationship with them.

There is no one correct way to show people kindness: it usually takes on whatever form makes sense to you, as long as the goal is to be considerate to someone else. It could take the form of doing the dishes for someone after they have cooked a meal for you or doing some charity work for others. It could even take on the form of simply understanding what they are going through and giving them your support.

For example, let us say that you and your friend have planned to go to dinner together and you were in the middle of getting ready. You get a call from your friend and she tells you she is having a panic attack because of something that happened at work and says she needs to cancel. You say it is fine, and you both hang up. In this situation, it would be natural to feel disappointed that your dinner got cancelled, as you were already getting dressed for it and were probably looking forward to some good food and good company.

However, to show kindness, instead of harboring any ill-feelings about the situation within yourself or expressing them to her, kindness means coming from a place of understanding and letting her know that you are there for her and will support her if she needs you. Saying these words to her will mean the world, as she will not feel guilty for having to cancel, and you would not have added to her existing anxiety. It is important though to also come from a place of understanding genuinely.

It is so easy to get caught up in your own emotions and needs such that sometimes you might forget that someone else may need your support and understanding during a tough time, even if it makes you feel a certain type of way. This would mean authentically understanding where your friend might be coming from and telling yourself that they need to focus on their needs right now. If this annoys you, try forgiving them and let the negativity go. Being kind is all about showing someone else that you are there for them and that you genuinely understand what their needs are without forcing your needs upon them.

Of course, if someone has wronged you in some way, you have the right to express how you feel and let them know how their actions affected you. No matter how kind you are, you still have the right to feel what you feel, however there is a fine line between letting those feelings cloud your judgment and pushing you to do something that may be deemed as unkind, and letting them know how their actions impacted you whilst expressing that you are willing to try and understand where they are coming from.

There are two sides of every story and in order to exuberant kindness, you need to understand both sides of the story. Ultimately, kindness is a state of being that helps you let go of any negative thoughts or emotions you might be harboring. Being genuinely kind to someone else, despite what you may be going through, makes you more selfless and makes the other person feel as though they can come to you with their vulnerabilities and feel supported.

Being kind to others means being authentically caring towards someone without expecting something in return. As easy as this may sound, oftentimes we do things with the expectation of having the favor returned at some point, however when we have this expectation we set ourselves up for disappointment. Not everybody expresses their gratitude in the same way and many times people may not repay you in the way that you wanted, and that is okay. Everybody is different, and it is unrealistic and unfair to expect everyone to conduct their lives the way you do. Expecting this from people will only hurt you and will make you think negatively about the relationships and friendships you have with people.

Setting expectations for each person you are kind to is not genuine kindness, and will leave you feeling miserable, which will leave you struggling to stay positive. Remind yourself that life is not about keeping score: it does not harm you to be kind to someone without expecting them to give you anything back. Being kind makes you feel positive about yourself and regardless of whether the other person recognizes it or even does something kind for you in return, your mind and heart will still feel lighter because you did a good thing for someone else. Kindness should not be rooted in resentment, but should be planted from a space of genuine selflessness, love and care.

Think of a time when someone acted a certain way with you that rubbed you the wrong way. What happened? Did you talk to that person about their side of the story?

_____
_____
_____

If you did talk to them about their side of the story, did you show them that you understood where they were coming from? Recount what happened:

_____
_____
_____

How do you usually show kindness to the world?

_____
_____
_____

Self-kindness

When we are not feeling positive within ourselves, it can be tough to show exuberant kindness to others while we are struggling to hone that kindness towards ourselves. When we are stuck in a zone where we are fighting internal battles, our minds get so consumed with the struggle itself that we get bogged down by feelings of frustration, anger, sadness and anxiety. Battling these emotions can make our mood and temperament particularly volatile, which can rub off the wrong way on other people. Our understanding of other people's situations gets narrower because we are so consumed with trying to understand our own situations and navigating how to solve our own problems first.

The trick here is to show yourself kindness and compassion. You are battling a lot right now, and it would not help if someone came into your life and started telling you that you are not strong enough or that you do not deserve to be happy. That would further push you down and make you feel as though you are unworthy of love and happiness and that your life will always be a struggle that will make you unhappy.

If you would not appreciate anybody telling you this at your lowest points, then why tell yourself those things? You are completely entitled to comfort yourself with kindness during the hard times, as you would for anybody else who is battling their own demons.

Your mind might automatically be inclined to criticize you for the way you are navigating your life, and the moment you try to defend yourself your mind starts to beat you down again. Sometimes, we can be so hard on ourselves for the most minute reasons and that really takes a toll on our confidence and mental health. Being hard on ourselves makes us feel worse about our life and it can make it very difficult to think positively. When we show kindness to ourselves, we are essentially telling ourselves to take a break from self-criticism. We are letting ourselves know that it is okay to not be perfect and that it is okay to battle our demons however we see fit – in effect, we are trying our best.

You are a strong woman, but it is important to remember that you will not have it all together every single minute of every day, and that is completely okay. The world will not fall apart if you need to fall apart. Give yourself the comfort you would like to receive from someone else - be your own mother. Sometimes, you might crave soothing reassurance and comfort, kind of like how a mother would comfort her child, and it is natural to want to be soothed this way because it makes you feel safe and supported. While you may have a wonderful support system, it is just as necessary to support yourself and so you need to be your own mother.

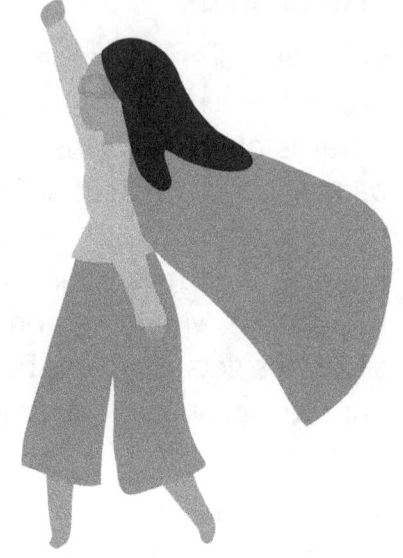

To self-soothe, start by identifying what emotions you are feeling and where those feel most heavy in your body. Are you feeling a lump in your throat? Are you feeling a knot in your stomach? Are you feeling heavy in your chest? Observe your mind and body and focus on where you are feeling most vulnerable. Once you channel your attention to that specific part (or parts) of the body, start by placing your hand on it. Lightly stroke that part of the body, as if you were stroking a child's head to make them fall back asleep after waking up from having a nightmare.

By stroking that part of your body you are physically soothing the area by transferring positive energy to it. While you are physically soothing, say kind words to yourself. As we have reiterated before, the way you talk to yourself matters and so showing yourself kindness means recognizing your strengths and telling yourself that you are doing your best. Being kind to yourself also means respecting yourself. Soothing yourself physically and verbally is a form of respect because you are giving yourself the attention you need to feel better, instead of shooting harsh words at yourself to bring you down. You deserve to be treated well, so do it for yourself, be understanding of the situation, and tell yourself the words that will uplift and comfort you.

When you are going through a tough time, what kind words could you say to yourself to show compassion?

_____

_____

_____

_____

_____

_____

_____

Being kind to yourself and others can make the world a better place. Your actions and kind words can have a huge positive impact on someone's day without you even knowing it. When you release positive energy in this manner, you feel positivity emerge within yourself. You feel happier, more confident and feel lighter within you. Kindness removes all of that negativity and toxicity that you might be harboring within you and dissipates that so you feel as though a weight has been lifted off your shoulders.

Positive emotions and thoughts are less energy-consuming than negative ones. Showing people you care for and understand them goes a long way in strengthening your bonds with others, plus you may even influence them to show kindness as well! We can all agree that having more people show kindness in the world would make the world a much better place to live in. When you are authentically compassionate towards yourself and other people, your thoughts will change from being harsh and negative to being more hopeful and considerate. Try it out!

What is one act of kindness you could do today for someone else?

_____

_____

_____

_____

_____

What is one act of kindness you can do for yourself?

_____

_____

_____

_____

_____

CHAPTER 9:
PRACTICE SELF-LOVE

Think about someone you love deeply. It could be a significant other, a family member or a friend. How do you usually express your love to them? Is it through physical touch such as hugging and kissing? Is it by telling them how amazing they are? Is it by washing the dishes for them when they are too tired to do it themselves? Now, think about what you love about this person. There must be reasons as to why you love this person so much and what keeps you drawn to them. As you are reflecting, you are probably feeling a rush of positive emotions about this person, which means you genuinely love this person and you think positively about this person.

Now, think about yourself. Are you feeling those same positive feelings and thoughts of love towards yourself? Chances are you probably are not. We are so conditioned to seeking validation, love and acceptance from external sources that we often forget to look for it within ourselves first. We are our biggest and most accessible source of validation, but our minds believe that validation from other people is somehow more impactful than validation from ourselves.

Directing the kind of love we give to other people towards ourselves as well can make us much happier people.

What does it mean to truly love ourselves? Self-love seems like such a vague concept and can be really hard to put into practice, especially if we are battling negative thought patterns. You probably come across various thoughts that bring you down throughout the day, rather than thoughts that lift you up, which can make it grueling to practice self-love and think positively. For something as little as stubbing your toe against a table leg, your mind could say something like "way to go, you hurt yourself yet again". It is so easy to be hard on ourselves instead of showing ourselves compassion. Self-love teaches you to treat yourself with the utmost respect and care that you deserve, and there are multiple ways you can go about practicing this.

List out all your amazing qualities

For some strange reason, we are able to easily see qualities within us that do not match our expectations rather than the wonderful qualities we do possess. This is probably because we are constantly comparing ourselves to other people's personalities and emphasizing our shortfalls based on their personality traits. It is important to remember that everybody has a holistic personality: no one is defined by just one trait.

Everybody has a huge cauldron of characteristics that make them unique, so it does not make sense to compare yourself to someone else because their personality combination is different to yours. In order to recognize your own amazing personality traits, you need to first stop comparing yourself to other people. Once you start to focus on yourself without making yourself feel bad for not meeting the benchmark that other people have set, you will start to make good progress in the practice of self-love.

Take time each day to go over the qualities that you love about yourself - these can be anything! It could be physical, mental, emotional, spiritual - whatever it is that you love about yourself! The goal here is to reflect back to yourself just how amazing you really are. To start off, you can write down all the good qualities you recognize within you on a piece of paper or in a virtual notepad on your phone.

Whatever method you choose to pen these traits down on, just be sure that you can access this list later, because you will have days when you are feeling miserable and need a little encouragement and validation from yourself; this is when that list comes handy.

Try writing down 10 amazing qualities you see in yourself below:

_____

_____

_____

_____

_____

_____

_____

Now that you have recognized and written down these qualities, look through them once again. Focus on each one. Read the quality, close your eyes and feel this quality fill you up. If one of your qualities is kindness, feel emotions and thoughts surrounding kindness fill you up and bask in that enriching feeling. Go through each good quality and make yourself believe that you embody every single one. These are the qualities that will make you feel confident about yourself and make you feel as though you can conquer the world.

Look through your list of awesome qualities every day and feel free to add more whenever you feel like it. Make it a habit to show yourself this list of qualities often enough so that you reach the point where you do not need to refer to this list and can automatically embrace all of these qualities on your own without feeling as though you are lying to yourself. The goal is to get to a place where you start saying encouraging things to yourself about yourself without it being an arduous task for you. The easier you can recognize just how amazing you are, the easier it becomes to genuinely love yourself.

Embrace your imperfections

Loving yourself means loving your whole self - that means the flaws too. While it is important to remind yourself of how awesome you truly are, it is also just as necessary to embrace your flaws so that you are not putting yourself down because of them. Every single person on this earth is a mixture of different qualities and every quality they embody makes them who they are. If we discount the flaws, then we are not looking at the person holistically and authentically. This includes us too.

Having flaws is not a bad thing, at all! Our flaws are what make us learn and grow into the people we want to be. Without flaws, we would have nothing to reflect on and nothing to work towards. The most enriching moments of our lives are when we are deep in self-reflection and reconnect with ourselves to heal through emotional wounds we may be carrying. No one is perfect, so embracing those flaws brings you multiple steps closer to truly loving yourself for who you are.

What you need to do here is change the association you have with your flaws. Oftentimes, you may think about all your weaknesses and get disgusted with yourself, wondering why you have these imperfect qualities. However, when you do this, you are choosing to perceive bits of yourself as negative or monstrous. Instead, you could change the association you have with these imperfections and think of them as learning paths.

If you were at a restaurant and you were served a plate of lasagna that was stone-cold, you would probably ask the server if they could send it back and heat it up for you. All you are doing is asking for your food to be served to you at the temperature you expected it to be served at and the chef is learning from this experience. There is no negativity here; it is a simple case of understanding and learning. Similarly, if you have an imperfection, you need to understand it and then learn how to grow from it while still accepting that you are not a bad person just because you have flaws. Take each imperfection as a reason to grow into the person you want to be.

This may be an emotional journey, but a necessary one. Introspect and write down whatever qualities you think are flaws in your eyes. List them down here:

_____

_____

_____

_____

_____

_____

_____

Now that you have listed your imperfections, go through each one and be compassionate with yourself when you think about each one. For example, if you noted down "low self-esteem" as one of your imperfections, take a deep breath and tell yourself that it is okay to have low self-esteem. Most of our imperfections are a part of us due to the experiences we have had in life, so be more considerate of yourself because chances are your imperfections have been a part of you due to some pain you have endured in the past.

Accept your flaws for what they are - manifestations of internal wounds that you have not healed yet. They are not monsters in your closet, they are parts of you that need attention and care so that they can be healed. Go through the list and breathe through the emotions you feel when you reflect on each one. Tell yourself that the imperfection is completely okay to have and that you are brave for trying to work on it.

Change the association you have with it from one of disappointment to one of curiosity and willingness to grow. Remind yourself that you are still an amazing person even with these imperfections and that it is definitely possible to use these flaws to your advantage to grow into the person you want to be. When you embrace your flaws, you lower the expectations you have for yourself to standards that are more realistic for you, which reduces the amount of self-doubt and self-criticism you would typically have. Your flaws start to look less threatening and feel like friendly parts of yourself that you will want to soothe and improve.

Look at the list of your imperfections above and write down how you can turn those into room for growth. What steps can you take to heal those wounds and work on turning those flaws into lessons?

Let go of toxicity

We touched upon this earlier, but removing toxic energy from your life is a surefire way of making space for positivity. If you are not sure what might be toxic in your life, take a step back and reflect on the parts of your life that make you unhappy. Are there particular aspects of your life that make you feel anxious, stressed, depressed, angry or sad?

Having negative associations with a certain event which leads to a one-off feeling is still okay - life is not perfect and there will be times when a certain part of your life will feel like it is falling apart.

Usually, there is a fix for this and if you are able to solve the problem without too much difficulty, then this is not considered to be toxic. However, if there is something in your life that is making you feel horrible on a regular basis and you feel as though there is no way out, this is a bold sign that this particular aspect of your life may be intertwined with toxicity and that toxic stimulus needs to be cut out. Toxicity might be coming from a relationship, a friendship, a job or even a behavior or thought process that you are embodying. The point is, something is considered toxic when it disguises itself as something beneficial for you when in actuality it is making your life very stressful.

For example, if a friend of yours constantly blames you for not being the ideal friend she wants you to be, even though you are an amazing person and are doing everything you can, then this is probably a toxic friendship. If you have a friend like this in your life, you probably feel more drained after meeting them than before meeting them, and this is not what constitutes a healthy friendship. Similarly, if there are other aspects of your life that are leaving you feeling horrible than how they should be making you feel, you need to let those go.

It will be tough at first, but letting go of anything toxic, no matter how close it is to you, will help push you further towards a space of positivity. When you harbor toxicity in your life, your energy becomes negative too and you are unable to attract the good things you truly deserve. Removing toxicity will make you realize just how much good you deserve and you will start to see your life fill up with happiness and peace, because your mind will feel more positive and will take action to bring in more positivity too.

Is there anything in your life that you think is toxic? What or who is it, and why?

___

___

___

___

___

How do you think you can remove this toxic stimulus from your life?

___

___

___

___

___

Take care of yourself

Loving yourself means taking care of your mind and body. In order to think positively and live a happy life, you need to be physically and mentally healthy. For your physical health, this means making sure you are eating a well-balanced diet, exercising regularly and maintaining a regular sleep cycle that gets you a good amount of sleep. Your body does so much for you, so it deserves to be treated like royalty. Do not allow your body to wear itself down, make sure that you are making the effort to nourish your body with the things that it needs in order to function properly and happily. If you are doing too much during the day that physically exerts you, be sure to give your body a break and let it rest and recuperate.

Our bodies are amazing because they can run on even the lowest amount of energy; however, they do have their breaking points as well and you do not want to reach a point where your body cannot keep up with your schedule. Your health is more important than anything else, so make sure you are giving your body the rest that it needs so that it can recharge and do everything you need it to do effectively.

In terms of your mental health, you need to take care of your mind as though you are a child. Sometimes, things can get so crazy that we forget to give our mind the mental nourishment it needs to calm down and relax. This could be anything from soaking in a warm bubble bath to reading a book you have not gotten a chance to read yet to simply applying a face mask and lighting some scented candles.

Meditation, as discussed earlier, is also an extremely effective way of bringing your mind to a standstill and simply just observing the present moment. Whatever you think you need to feel mentally nourished again, give yourself exactly that. You deserve to feel at peace, but sometimes life gets in the way and it can be difficult to prioritize doing things that make you truly happy.

It is essential for you to give yourself the things you need in order to feel taken care of, because taking care of yourself will make you feel empowered and more balanced. You have the right to spoil and pamper yourself as much as you need in order to feel loved.

If you are going through something heavy right now, speaking to a therapist is also a form of care, because you get to talk about your issues and seek guidance from a professional, instead of keeping everything bottled up inside and reliving the same unhealthy thought patterns and behaviors. Providing yourself with the space to vent to a therapist is a form of self-care that will reap benefits because this is a form of care that will guide you towards the right path of healing, so do not ever think that you have to do this alone.

What are some things you can do to take care of your physical health?

_____

_____

_____

_____

What are some things you can do to take care of your mental health?

_____

_____

_____

_____

Go after what you want

Oftentimes, we let the fear of failure or judgment from others keep us from going after the things we truly want, however this is a form of self-betrayal. You are denying yourself a potentially awesome life because of an internal fear of the possibility that something might go wrong. If you are a mother, imagine your child wanting to start taking art classes because this is something they really want to try because they enjoy it and have a knack for painting.

You know how much they would get out of these classes but you say no to them because you fear that they will fail, and of course, your child gets extremely upset and you feel guilty that you denied them a chance of pursuing something that could make them happy. In reality, you most probably would not deny them this opportunity and would do everything you can to support their dream. Similarly, you also deserve to be taken care of, so do not say no to yourself when you want to chase after a dream that might seem far-fetched. Give your inner child what she deserves to be happy.

You can do this by thinking about what it is that makes you happy - do you like being artsy? Do you like learning new skills? Have you wanted to increase your income and start a new business or invest? Do you like being physically active? Think about what makes you feel the most like yourself and go after what you want. Set goals for yourself and spend the time and energy needed to achieve them, because chances are you will not regret it.

That sense of accomplishment you feel for making the effort to realize your dreams will reconfigure your mindset to be more motivated, which will ultimately lead to a more positive mindset. Going after what you want is the most genuine form of self-love because you are not neglecting your needs, and that will make you feel so much more positive once you start to see your life change because of it.

What have you always wanted to do but never taken the step to do?

___

___

___

___

What steps can you take now to start chasing that dream?

___

___

___

___

By when do you want to have achieved that goal or that dream? Set a deadline for yourself.

___

___

___

___

Reconnect with yourself

Last but not least, spend time with yourself alone. For other people to enjoy your presence, you need to be able to enjoy your own presence first. You are an amazing woman who is constantly evolving as your life goes on - why not take the time to get to know this evolved you on a deeper level? As cliché as this is, go for long walks at the beach and stare out into the sunset while you're introspecting about your life.

Take the time to ask yourself uncomfortable questions that you never got a chance to ask yourself so that you can learn what emotional baggage you are still carrying around.

Doing this paves the way for genuine self-healing, which can help you build a life for yourself that you find more fulfilling, instead of hiding behind those emotional shadows. Doing new things can also bring you some enriching experiences that can show you sides of yourself that you normally might not have been aware of. You could find out you have a certain talent or you can find out that you have a phobia of something. You feel closer to yourself and end up seeing just how beautiful you are on the inside as well as on the outside. You realize how much you truly deserve and you start to go after things that make you genuinely happy.

Being one with yourself again gives you an authentic view of who you truly are, and you can more easily love yourself for who you are rather than for what you pretend to be, which eradicates all the stress you may otherwise feel trying to be someone you are not.

What can you do to reconnect with yourself?

_____

_____

_____

_____

_____

How often will you take the time to reconnect with yourself?

_____

_____

_____

_____

Over the course of this book, have you reconnected with yourself? What have you learned about yourself?

_____

_____

_____

_____

_____

CONCLUSION

Hopefully, this book has given you more insight into what it means to have a positive mindset and how to get there. Remember that you are a beautiful, amazing and caring woman who deserves the world, so do not ever forget that. All of the tools this book has provided you will get you much closer to thinking positively, no matter how hard life might seem. With the exercises you did throughout, you also have a better understanding of how to thoroughly introspect in a manner that gives you helpful learnings about yourself which you can work on to improve the areas of your life that you find dissatisfying.

Positive thinking means gaining the courage to make changes, and you are already there. By completing this workbook, you have taken a huge step towards changing your life, so do not stop here! Take the lessons that you have learned in this book and apply it to your real life. It will not be a cakewalk, but with practice and determination, you will be able to change your outlook on life to a more positive one than you had before. Good luck on your journey of positivity - do not worry, you got this!

AUTHOR'S NOTE

Dear reader, I hope you enjoyed my book.

Please don't forget to toss up a quick review on amazon, I will personally read it! Positive or negative, I'm grateful for all feedback.

Reviews are so helpful for self-published authors and your feedback can make such a difference for my book!

Thanks very much for your time, and I look forward to hearing from you soon.

Sincerely,

Victoria

www.ingramcontent.com/pod-product-compliance
Lightning Source LLC
Chambersburg PA
CBHW081349080526
44588CB00016B/2430